GRACE MULLIGAN'S

DUNDEE·KITCHEN

COOK BOOK

Published by DUNDEE 800, Dundee 1991
Printed by David Winter & Son Ltd., Dundee

CONTENTS

FOREWORD

Shortly after my arrival in Dundee in the spring of 1990, a spritely little lady called Mrs McGlynn knocked on my door and said, 'I read about *Dundee 800* and I have a daughter who is a famous cook and author. I'm sure she'd by happy to help celebrate Dundee's Octocentenary.'

Some months later I had the pleasure of meeting Grace Mulligan and, like millions of her TV viewers of Yorkshire TV's Farmhouse Kitchen, was charmed by her warm personality and engaging sense of humour. When Grace agreed to write a cookbook of Dundee recipes and reminiscences I was delighted.

I am sure this unique publication will not only evoke memories and creative activity in the kitchens of Dundee, but that it will find a place in the heart and hearth of all those who enjoy good homespun fare for the next 800 years.

Henny King
Director
Dundee 800

GRACE MULLIGAN

Grace Mulligan's own name is Donnelly and she was born and brought up in Dundee, where most of her family still live. From St. Patrick's Primary School she went on to Lawside Academy, and from there to the Edinburgh College of Domestic Science, and Moray House Teacher Training College in Edinburgh's Royal Mile. Back in her home town, Grace taught at St. John's Secondary School for three years in the large Domestic Science Department there. The big house, now demolished, looked out on to the Nethergate almost opposite the Queen's Hotel. Jessie Duncan was Head of Department, and she, as a very young teacher, had been a member of "The Committee of Dundee Domestic Science Teachers" who put together "The Dundee Homecraft Book" which became the cookery bible for all Dundee Schools. This lovely little blue paperback is not just for recipes and cookery advice, its chapters also include laundry and housewifery.

Grace met her husband, Brian, when they were both in Edinburgh. He was a medical student from the Lang Toon – Kirkcaldy. After their marriage they set about looking for a practice, not an easy job then. Sadly they had to leave Scotland to take up a job in Yorkshire, where they have been ever since. This was before the days of Health Centres and secretaries, and a doctor and his wife in General Practice were very busy indeed. The small town of Goole had three small hospitals and a Maternity Home. There were, however, no resident doctors in any of these hospitals. The local doctors had to take on responsibilities in the various departments, looking after admissions, supervising patients after operations from visiting consultants. On top of all this the Casualty Department had to be manned day and night. Life was hectic, especially when four children came along – one son and three daughters.

It was when Grace and Brian moved to a bigger house in the village of Hook, just outside Goole, that Grace joined the village Women's Institute, which had just been formed. The Women's Institute is run in much the same way as the W.R.I. in Scotland. It was through her association, first with the local W.I., and later with the Yorkshire County Federation, that Grace was invited to study to become a cookery judge. Eventually Grace was elected to the Executive Committee in York, and later became a member of the National Association Home Economics Committee in London. Every year the Yorkshire Federation, with its 230 institutes, organised an exhibition at their pavilion at the Great Yorkshire Show in Harrogate. This is, of course, an agricultural show, very much like the Highland Show in Edinburgh. Grace often demonstrated there in both the cookery and handicraft sections. In fact, it was through her work at this show that her name was given to Mary Watt, the producer of Farmhouse Kitchen. Mary and her husband, Graham, have produced and directed the series right from the beginning. Grace appeared as guest cook with Dorothy Sleightholme, the then presenter, for four or five programmes. Shortly after, Dorothy, who had done the programme for twelve years, retired, and Grace was invited to take her place as regular presenter.

Farmhouse Kitchen is the longest running cookery programme on television. It is now twenty-one years old. It was made by Yorkshire Television, one of the "Big Five" I.T.V. companies. It has been a national programme for all of its twenty-one years. The idea for the programme came from a man called Donald Baverstock. It was also his idea to start a series about a farm in Yorkshire. This, of course, is Emmerdale Farm. In fact, Farmhouse Kitchen and Emmerdale, until recently, were broadcast from the same studio. It was quite usual to see Annie's kitchen going up when Farmhouse Kitchen was coming down.

The Farmhouse Kitchen series consists of thirteen programmes, each lasting for about 30 minutes. Grace does about six programmes on her own, and the rest with a guest. This might be a specialist like the fish restauranteur, Rick Stein, from Padstow in Cornwall. Rick did some very exotic fish dishes and Grace did starters and puddings to complement his food. Other guests might be specialists from a food industry, like the girl who worked for the Potato Marketing Board, or the home economist from the British Diabetic Association, or the representative from the Sea Fish Authority in Edinburgh. There were occasional "stars," like the head chef from the Ritz Hotel, and on a Christmas programme, the cookery author Josceline Dimbleby.

In 1988 the programme won the Glenfiddich Award for the best cookery programme on T.V. These awards are subsidised by Wm. Grant, the distillers from Banffshire, and were founded overy twenty-one years ago. That same year, Farmhouse Kitchen won the overall award for excellence in promoting good, honest food. This was particularly gratifying because the other eleven categories came from other T.V. food programmes from the B.B.C. and radio, food journalists from the national and local press; writers from food sections in magazines, etc. etc. It was a great year for the team, since the names engraved on the silvery trophy are some of our most distinguished food writers – Elizabeth David, Jane Grigson, and Derek Cooper himself who was, in fact, chairman of the judging panel that year. In his speech Derek, who presents the Radio Four food programme, said that Farmhouse Kitchen was unashamedly instructive, and full of good, sensible advice.

Grace is now a well-known author. There are nine books associated with the programme – six paperbacks and two big hardbacks. She is a regular contributor to the Yorkshire Post and many magazines like Woman, Woman and Home, Freezer Digest, T.V. Times, and SAGA magazine. A recent extension of her work has been as a presenter of videos commissioned by various organisations. A recent one was made for the Osteoporosis Society to heighten public awareness of the condition. Wendy Craig did the opening poem, Lizzie Webb did the exercise bit, Anita Harris did the exercise bit in the swimming pool, and Grace did the nutrition bit about which foods are best for the condition.

Grace finds that answering letters from viewers is very rewarding. People go to enormous trouble sometimes and the letters can be long and complicated, full of questions, opinions, and compliments too. Letters come from abroad in the English speaking countries where the programe is shown. South African viewers send some wonderful letters, and Grace is probably going out there under the auspices of a woman's magazine.

Being on T.V. Grace is in constant demand for opening Garden Fêtes, Christmas Bazaars, and supermarkets! She is also much sought after as an after dinner/lunch speaker. However, despite the pleasures of her life on the fringe of show business it is still as great a pleasure for Grace to come home to "Bonnie Dundee," and see it thriving and blossoming as the City of Discovery which is preparing itself for the twenty-first century.

INTRODUCTION

The idea for this book came from Henny King – Director of Dundee 800. It is one of many events taking place this year to celebrate the birth of Dundee 800 years ago.

I have greatly enjoyed putting together recipes of the Dundee I remember and reminiscing about my home town. It is not at all a comprehensive list of the recipes I could have written to cover all aspects of Scottish food. I have made several programmes on Scottish dishes in my television cookery series Farmhouse Kitchen and they were very well received, particularly in commonwealth countries.

Dundee must be unique in having two world-famous dishes named after it – *Dundee Marmalade and Dundee Cake.* Did you know that Cary Grant offered tea and a "slice of Dundee Cake" to his beautiful co-star in the famous film "An American in Paris"?

I have searched in vain for a reference to food in the works of Dundee's poet William McGonagall. He just did not seem interested in food – probably far too mundane for him. However, a McGonagall expert did tell me that William once approached a pie man and offered him a poem in exchange for a pie. Sad to say the pie man refused. I did, however, see Blind Mattie once, playing her squeeze-box and singing outside Wallace's Bakery in Dura Street. A white coated girl came out of the shop and gave her a paper bag with a pie and a cake in it. Blind Mattie thanked her warmly with a big gummy grin, put her back against the wall, and slid to the ground to eat her pie. I'll never forget her look of utter contentment, or her tattered clothes and boots.

Some Dundee people have no idea they live in such a beautiful place. Its situation on the Tay is breathtaking. I am proud to be a Dundonian. As for food, I am usually laden for my journey south at the end of a visit. In my bag there is always a plain loaf – Curly Kate, and Plain Geordie have a taste of their own – White puddings, Smokies, and Chocolate Violets. All of them remind me of my happy days in Dundee, and all the extra friends I have made through television. I have been very blessed.

I would very much like my warmest thanks to be recorded to Avril Evans of Goole, England, for typing all my recipes and for her patience with all the "foreign" words she dealt with.

My thanks also to my eldest daughter, Catriona, who did the line drawings.

NB. Anyone using a fan assisted oven should note that the oven temperatures in these recipes should be reduced by 10 degrees (10°) or in accordance with instruction booklet which came with the cooker.

RECIPES

Dundee Broth

Any Scot worthy of the name can make a good pot of soup, broth or kail. All three names mean much the same thing – a soup with some meat and a mixture of dried and fresh vegetables. The soup pot in our house is always called the kail pot. The name seems to have come from the use of green vegetable kale. I do not remember when my mother got rid of her iron kail pot in favour of a bright aluminium one. Dundee readers of the "Tele" sent me a beauty, as well as a lovely smooth girdle, to use on my programme. My mother found a long-handled iron stew pot in Dens Road market, and I have used all three old utensils in several Scottish programmes. The meat for the broth can be something like thick flank beef, or neck of lamb, hough, or just beef bones, or even better, bacon bones. I like to tie the meat up, even if it is just a small piece. It is then easy to fish out after it is cooked in order to separate and discard all the fat. The meat is then chopped small to return to the soup. You can use a bigger piece of meat, which is then served with potatoes and vegetables as the second course after the broth. This gives you a one pot meal. The dried peas and barley need to soak in water overnight, or for at least four hours.

2 oz (50 g) dried green peas
2 oz (50 g) barley
2 oz (50 g) yellow split peas
5 pints (2.8 litres) water
1½ lbs (675 g) piece of beef
or lamb. Beef bones or
bacon bones
8 oz (225 g) diced carrots
4 oz (125 g) diced turnip
4 oz (125 g) chopped kale
or cabbage
2 oz (50 g) chopped leeks
1 tbsp chopped parsley
Salt and pepper

Soak the first three ingredients overnight in water, or for at least four hours. Next day drain them through a sieve and add to the five pints of water. Stir well and add all the other ingredients, except the salt, pepper and parsley. Bring to a boil, turn the heat down, and simmer for 1½-2 hours depending on how much meat. Remove meat, discard fat and chop the meat very small. Stir into the soup. Taste, season, and add fresh parsley at last minute.

Soup Pot

SMOKIES

Smokies

I made a film recently for B.B.C. Scotland at the But & Ben Restaurant at Auchmithie, near Arbroath. Margaret and Ian Horn made our crew very welcome, and I learned a bit more about the history of the Smokie from Margaret whose family name – Spink – is one of the famous fishing families of Arbroath. I didn't know that the thick navy woollen skirts the fishwives wore were called "coats." In the 1930's they used to come by the old L.N.E.R. rail link to Dundee, just twenty miles away, with their picturesque costumes and heavy creels. Their warm outfits were strictly practical for their hard working lives. The heavy skirts were long and seemed to me to have one or two layers underneath as well. On top was a blouse and over that a tightly held shawl crossed at the front and pinned at the back. The creels must have been heavy, even without the wet fish inside. These sturdy women, with their ruddy complexions, travelled all over Dundee by tram. I remember seeing them at the old tram stop opposite the Kings Picture House, having trudged up Trades Lane from the station. Reaching our part of town at Stobswell they still had to climb up and down the stone tenement stairs to reach their customers. The heavy creels were strapped to their backs with the webbing across the front of their shoulders. If the creel was really heavy the webbing strap might be across their foreheads, their backs bent to take the strain. They sold smokies, and white fish too, but I have no recollection of how much my mother paid. I only remember the strong east coast accent and wonderful taste of the fish they sold.

I don't remember ever doing anything with the Smokies, like making savoury quiches, or paté, as we do today. We ate them hot in winter and cold in summer, but, of course, we made soup with the stock made from the skins and bones. Our local fish shop in Albert Street, opposite Eliza Street, was almost next to Barrie's Lemonade factory. We used to buy Barrie's milk there too – we would call it long life milk now. Fish was an important part of our diet, either lightly stewed in milk or dressed in breadcrumbs and fried. "Dressed Herrings" – Dundee's answer to an economical first footing gift – were a sight to see in the week prior to Hogmanay. The usually austere white-tiled fish shop was festooned with kippered herrings "dressed" in coloured crepe paper bow ties and frills. There was a fish lady too who sat at the foot of the Hilltown selling "wulks" and dulse at a ha'penny a bag. The dulse was already boiled and doused in vinegar. It is funny to see it emerging as a "healthy" food in today's smart restaurants.

A Hot Smokie

A really fresh Smokie is very fragile. To open it up I find it easiest to support the backbone and squeeze gently from the open side. Now lay the fish flat on a heat proof plate, open it fully to remove the bones. Dot a little butter here and there and slip the plate under a hot grill. Watch carefully as it soon burns and dries up. The easiest way of all is to heat the fish in a microwave oven for about one and a half minutes, on full power (depending on size). Put another plate over the smokie to help stop the fishy smell sticking to the inside of your microwave.

Luxury Smokie Soup

Never throw away the skin or bones of a Smokie. Even if you are not going to make the soup straight away you can make a little stock and freeze it. Just put the skin and bones into a pot and barely cover with water. Bring to a boil and simmer for about 20 minutes, strain and discard the bones, etc., and freeze the fishy stock. Another method is to freeze skins and bones until you have enough for a big pot full. For this luxury Smokie soup I am using two whole fish.

2 medium sized Smokies
2 lbs (900 g) potatoes, peeled and cut into chunks
1 lb (450 g) onions, peeled and chopped
White pepper
1 large tbsp. chopped parsley
4/5 tblsp. single cream

Prepare two Smokies as described above. Set aside the flaked fish but put the skins and bones in a pot with water to cover. Simmer for 20 minutes. Meanwhile put the potatoes and onions in another pot and barely cover with water and cook until soft. Strain both the fishy liquid and the potatoes and onions, but do not throw away the liquid. Into a food processor put the fish, the fishy liquid and the soft potatoes and onions. Process until smooth, adjust the thickness with the reserved potato and onion water. Taste and adjust the seasoning. Stir in the parsley and serve very hot with a swirl of cream in each bowl.

(N.B. a food processor or liquidiser makes short work of this recipe.)

Smoked Haddock Soup

The yellow of this fish gives the soup a delicate gold colour.

1½ lbs (675 g) smoked haddock pieces (or cod)
8 oz (225 g) onions, peeled and finely chopped
1 pint (600 ml) milk
Very smooth hot mashed potoato (I have used reconstituted dried potato pieces very successfully)
1 oz (25 g) butter
Salt and white pepper

Put the smoked fish in a pot with the onion and barely cover with water. Simmer for five to ten minutes, or until the fish is done. Lift the fish and onion out of the water. Skin and de-bone the fish carefully, chop it and set aside. Meanwhile prepare the potatoes and be sure they are smooth and creamy. Gradually add the fish stock and milk to the soft potatoes. Adjust the seasoning with pepper and salt. Reheat and stir in the butter, smoked haddock and onion. Serve very hot.

"Cherry" of the Tay – The Sparling

This is not a pudding, but the nickname of the Sparling – a fish which is regularly fished in the River Tay. I was astonished to hear all about it from Charlie Johnson of Newburgh. We did a filmed interview for BBC Scotland and Charlie said that this fish lost popularity at the time of the First World War. He still sells it regularly to two ports – Liverpool and St. Ives.

To celebrate *DUNDEE 800* a Dundee-based chef, Jacob Chacko, of the Royal Oak, 167 Brook Street, Dundee, has decided to keep the Sparling on his menu for a year. Charlie and I ate the fish cooked in three different ways in his restaurant:

1. Cleaned and dipped in oatmeal and fried and served with lemon.

2. Cleaned and dipped in flour and fried, then seasoned very well.

3. I suggested this last method because the fish looks to me like a large sardine and so we tried it cooked under a fierce grill like a sardine. It was delicious with a squeeze of lemon juice and brown bread and butter.

Osmerus Esperlanus is the Sparling's proper name and one of its distinguishing features is that, when very fresh, it smells like cucumber!! In England the fish is known by another name still – the common European Smelt – but whatever its name it came as a great surprise to me that the Tay produces a fish I'd never heard of. It would be nice to hope it again becomes popular because of *DUNDEE 800*.

Sweet Pickled Herring

(Start four days before you need them)

My mother dislikes herring, so we never had any when I was young. However, an uncle of mine enjoyed cooking (and he was thought to be very strange because of this) and he used to make pickled herring. This recipe is a very nice sweet pickled herring with no skin or bones. It is a variation on a recipe we used on a Farmhouse Kitchen programme. It came from my right-hand helper and friend, Margaret Heywood. Margaret supervises all the food preparation which has to go on before the programme starts.

4 fl oz (120 ml) white vinegar
4 fl oz (120 ml) white wine
or cider vinegar
4 fl oz (120 ml) water
3 oz (75 g) granulated sugar
1 small onion, peeled and
finely sliced
White pepper
3 Allspice berries & 3 cloves
Pinch of fennel seed
Pickling liquor
3 fat herrings
Salt

Stir together all the ingredients, except the herring and salt. Ask the fishmonger to clean the herring. Top and tail and remove as many bones as possible. Cut each herring into two fillets and check carefully that all the bones are out. Sprinkle dry salt (about 1 tablespoon) into a shallow dish. Arrange one single layer of fish on top. Add another layer of salt, then fish, ending with a layer of salt. Cover tightly with a lid or foil. Leave in a cold place for 2 days. Remove the herring from the salt and peel off the skin. You will find the fish has gone quite stiff. When the skin is off there will still be a pearly sheen left behind. Soak the herring in water for about an hour. Pat the fillets dry with kitchen paper. Replace in a clean dish and pour over the liquor. Cover and leave for 48 hours in a cold place.

Serve the herring chopped into a potato salad as a starter or leave whole and serve simply with brown bread and butter and fresh tomato slices.

Crispy Herring

2 herring, cleaned (tops,
tails and bones removed)
Medium oatmeal (2 tblsp.)
1 oz butter
1 tblsp. oil
Salt and pepper

Pat the herring dry and press into the dry oatmeal. Melt the butter and oil in a large frying pan or grill. Cook the herring, first on one side then the other, for about 3/4 mins. each side, or longer if the fish is thick. Drain quickly on kitchen paper. Season with salt and pepper and serve at once.

Golden Cutlets

My mother always just poached these lovely, lightly-smoked fish in a milk and water mixture. They are very quick to cook, and even quicker in a microwave. Traditionally they were supposed to be served with a poached egg on top of each one.

4 small smoked haddock
Milk and water mixed to
 cover (about ½ pint)
White pepper

Rinse in cold water and lay the fish in the bottom of a shallow pot or frying pan. Season with pepper and pour over the milk and water mixture. Cover with a lid and cook very gently for about 8/10 mins. Serve with creamy potatoes mashed with butter and some of the liquid from the fish pan.

KERRS
PINKS

Mince and Tatties

Mince and tatties with neeps or carrots must have been the basis of millions and millions of dinners for Scots families for centuries. This simple meal is easy, fast, and tasty. First of all buy the best quality mince you can get. Look for minced beef with less fat and which has been freshly minced. Notice I do not say look for meat with no fat at all, which will give you a dish with little flavour. Some fat is necessary for taste. For a perfect result cook the mince and eat it on the day you buy it. Raw mince should not be left in a 'fridge for more than one day in my opinion. You can freeze both raw and cooked mince but try to use it wihin two-three weeks. As for texture, I do not care for the very finely minced beef from one of the famous stores. The final dish has no texture at all. Try to find a butcher who will mince rather more coarsely for you. Of course, you must not ask him in the middle of a hectic Friday morning, rather give him notice so that he can have it ready for you.

Choose your potatoes with care as well. Some waxy potatoes do not mash well. My mother's favourite were Kerr's pinks, but we only got these on high days and holidays. Root vegetables, hard as rocks, were another staple. Bashed neeps (mashed turnips) are a sloppy mess once you have mashed them but set them in a nylon sieve to drain. Once they have shed a lot of liquid beat with plenty of pepper and melted butter. Freshly grated nutmeg is a good addition but flavour gently at first until you decide if it's for you. Top and tail carrots, then scrape or scrub, chop in good sized chunks for good flavour. Aim for them to be just cooked and no more. You can thicken mince in the old way with medium oatmeal or with plain flour mixed to a thin paste with cold water.

Rich Mince

2 lb (900 g) best quality
   minced beef
3 medium onions, peeled
   and chopped
3 medium carrots, peeled
   and sliced
Water or meat stock made
   with a cube
1 large tbsp. of medium
   oatmeal (or 1 large tbsp.
   plain flour mixed to a
   paste with a little water)
Spot of gravy salt to colour
Pepper

As soon as you can, use a large heavy based pan to fry the mince. Do this over a high heat. You should not need extra fat. It might stick at first but keep on stirring. The high heat caramelises the meat juices which in turn will give a good gravy. This could take about twenty minutes. Take the mince out of the pan and start to fry the onions (you may need an extra knob of fat at this point). After just a few minutes put the meat and carrots in the pan with the onions. Stir well and add enough water or stock to cover the meat and no more. Turn the heat down to a simmer for about twenty minutes. Thicken the mince with either the spoonful of oatmeal or the flour slaked in a little water. Keep stirring until the mince thickens, add a dot of gravy salt to improve the colour and stir in pepper to taste.

Skirlie

Oatmeal, dripping and onions are the three ingredients for Skirlie. It is a versatile accompaniment for mince and tatties. It also works well as a stuffing for all sorts of meat and chicken dishes. It is said to be called Skirlie because of the noise it makes in the frying pan while cooking – just like the skirl of the pipes! It's a lovely story, I hope it is true. Well-flavoured dripping makes all the difference to this simple dish. Bacon fat is particularly good.

2 oz (50 g) good dripping or
   bacon fat
1 lb (450 g) onions, peeled
   and sliced
4 oz (125 g) medium oatmeal
   (or pinhead)
Salt and pepper

Melt the fat in a heavy frying pan and fry the onions for a minute or two, then stir in the oatmeal. Stir constantly over a medium heat. If you are using pinhead meal you may have to add a little warm water at this point to keep it from sticking. Adjust the seasoning with salt and pepper. How long you go on frying depends on how "nutty" you like the finished Skirlie. I prefer the coarse texture, so mine comes off the heat once the onions are well done. If you want the oatmeal really soft, add a little more water and go on cooking.

Meat Roll

I often see straight sided pottery jars in fancy kitchenware shops with the words "Meat Roll" stamped on the side. I wonder if they are ever used to make a good old-fashioned meat roll. It is very economical and with a sharp knife it goes a long, long way. It is nice hot, cut in thick slices, and served with fried onion rings. Cold, it is excellent in sandwiches or with a salad and a good home-made chutney. Ours used to be steamed in our deep kail pot. It can also be cooked in water in a pressure cooker or baked in the oven in a loaf tin. Cover the tin with foil and set it in a roasting tin with 2/3 inches of water. This is a water bath, or a "bain-marie" as the French say.

1 lb (450 g) best steak mince
1 lb (450 g) streaky bacon,
 de-rinded
8 oz (225 g) onions, peeled
 and finely chopped
6 oz (175 g) rolled oats
2 tblsp. Worcester sauce
2 teasp. made up mustard
2 medium eggs, beaten
½ pint (300 ml) water or
 meat stock
For serving cold:
2 oz (50 g) dried
 breadcrumbs

Chop the bacon into small pieces. This is easier with a pair of scissors. Put the meat, bacon, onions, oats, sauce and mustard in a large mixer, add the beaten eggs and mix. If the mixture looks dry add water or stock to make a soft mixture. Pack into the meat jar, leaving 1" (5cm) space at the top. Cover with foil and steam in a deep pan with water half way up the sides of the jar. Steam for 2½ hours. Allow to cool then remove the roll from the jar. If you wish to serve it cold, dry off the surface with kitchen paper then roll the meat in the bread-crumbs.

Potted Hough

(Jellied Meat)

The rich, full flavour of a good potted hough is hard to beat. The drawback is that it takes six hours to cook. A pressure cooker would cut that time to two hours. I do remember buying hough in a tiny shop near my Granny's house in Kinloch Street. You handed in your own bowl the day before. I see in many Scottish cookery books it says that its jellied goodness makes a lovely summer salad. I'm sure it does, but it is infinitely better with a mound of creamy mashed potatoes, and a piece of potted hough melting gently in the middle. Some butchers still make their own hough. It is easy, but wait until you expect a crowd to make the most of it, or melt it down for the basis of a wonderful rich soup.

3 lbs (1.3 kg) hough or shin of beef (cut small)
1 knee bone or knuckle bone
Blade of mace
3 whole cloves

Rinse the hough and bones and place in a large pan with water to cover. Add spices and one shake of salt and pepper. Cover, bring to a boil. Turn down heat to a simmer for about six hours, or until the meat is falling apart. Remove meat and bones and allow to cool. Separate the meat from the gristle and bone, and chop it small. Set aside, covered. Strain off the liquor and leave to set overnight. Remove fat from surface. If the water beneath has not set to a firm jelly, re-boil uncovered to reduce volume further. Stir in meat and pour into wetted bowls and pots. Set aside to firm up.

Stovies

Like many Dundonians I remember Stovies with affection. My mother used to do hers in a heavy iron stewpan with a tin lid. The trouble is the recipes differ wildly, and no two are alike. My version uses good-quality dripping. In some parts of the east coast butchers sell what they call "Stovie Dripping." This is dripping with a good thick layer of meat juices under the set fat. This is what is left after roasting a piece of beef which is to be eaten cold and therefore the meat residue is not used for gravy. If you haven't got that kind of dripping you could use just a touch of gravy salt, or even left over gravy. Some people like, at the last minute, to stir in some chopped cooked meat: Corned beef is good.

1 lb (450 g) potatoes (not the waxy ones) peeled and sliced
1 lb (450 g) onions, peeled and sliced
2 oz (50 g) good Stovie dripping
Salt and pepper
Left over gravy or gravy salt (optional)
Stock from a meat cube
Parsley or chives (optional)

Put the Stovie dripping in a hevy pan with a good tight lid. Allow it to become very hot. Add the sliced onions and turn down the heat. Stir well then add the sliced potatoes. Again mix well to coat the potatoes with the flavoured fat. Season with salt and pepper (at this point stir in the left over gravy or gravy salt if you wish). Now add a little stock (made from a meat cube) and cook on a very low heat with the lid on for 1-2 hours or until the potatoes are soft. The idea is to cook the potatoes with as little liquid as possible. Shake the pan every now and then adding just a touch of stock to keep them from sticking. Some people like to raise the heat at the end of cooking in order to scorch the potatoes slightly while stirring all the time so that the Stovies are flecked with crispy bits. Serve very hot with parsley or chives scattered on top.

Desperate Dan's Cow Peh (Pie)

Dundee steak pies are nearly always bought ready made. They are traditionally topped with very flaky pastry and are rectangular. I have checked that Desperate Dan's Cow Peh (pie) is always round. A pie dish or tin should have a good "lip." It is then easier to seal the pastry and knock up and decorate the outside edge. This is usually done with scallops but I think Dan would feel this was a very cissy thing to do so we'll keep this pie very plain. The 2 lb (900 g) of meat can be all stewing beef if you wish, but I like the addition of a little hough for extra flavour. You will need a pie dish or tin with about 2½ pints (1.5 litre) capacity.

Suet Pastry:

12 oz (325 g) self raising white flour
1½ teasp. baking powder
¼ teasp. each dried thyme and sage
¼ teasp. salt
6 oz (175 g) suet (packet)
1 large egg
2 tblsp. water

Sift the flour and baking powder into a mixing bowl. Stir in the dried herbs, salt and suet. Beat together the egg and the water and use enough of the mixture to mix a fairly firm dough. Knead lightly in the bowl until smooth. Set aside covered until you need it.

Pie Filling:

2 oz (50 g) dripping or two tblsp. oil
1¾ lbs (800 g) stewing steak cut in chunks
4 oz (125 g) hough cut in small pieces
6 oz (175 g) ox kidney cut small
1 large onion peeled and chopped
2 medium carrots peeled and chopped
2 tblsp. plain white flour
1 pint (600 ml) beef stock made with a cube
Salt and pepper
Gravy browning or gravy salt

Check over the meat and kidney. Remove all skin and some fat. Skin and core the kidney and cut small. Using a roomy pan brown the meats and kidney in the dripping (oil). You may have to do this in two batches. Do this over a fairly high heat, stirring all the time. Remove the meat and kidney from the pan and fry the onion and carrots for a few minutes. You may have to use more dripping or oil. Put the browned meat and kidney back in the pan with the vegetables. Sprinkle the flour on top with salt and pepper. Add enough stock to barely cover the meat and kidney etc. Season with salt and pepper. Bring to a boil then reduce to a simmer for about two hours or until the meat is really tender. Stir with care to avoid breaking up the meat. Add a little gravy browning or gravy salt to darken the colour if you wish. Leave aside to go cold.

To assemble the pie:

Roll out the pastry on a floured board to about ½ inch (1 cm) thick, and about 1 inch wider than the dish. Remove any settled fat on the cooked meat with a slotted spoon. Transfer the meat, kidney, and vegetables to the pie dish. Add just enough gravy to keep the meat moist and position a pie funnel in the middle of the dish to hold up the pastry as it cooks. Now cut a 1 inch (2.5 cm) strip from the outside edge of the rolled out pastry, long enough to fit round the pie dish. Wet the rim of the pie dish with water and press the strip all round it. Wet the upperside of the strip, lift the pastry with your rolling pin and cover the pie. Press the edges very firmly to get a good seal. Lift the pie carefully in your left hand and trim off the excess pastry angling your knife with the handle under the dish. Use a fork to press the outside of the edges together again and make a neat steam hole over the pie funnel. Brush the pastry with beaten egg or milk and set the pie on a baking sheet. Bake at Gas 7, 425°F, 220°C, for about 30-40 minutes or until the pastry is crisp and brown. Reheat the extra gravy, adding more stock to give a generous amount.

Pot Roast Brisket

I do not remember us ever roasting beef in the oven at home – it was much more likely to be a pot roast of fresh brisket. Vegetables were dropped into the pot about 20 minutes before we intended eating, and meat, vegetables and gravy were all ready together. Only potatoes had to be cooked on their own.

3-3½ lb (1.3 to 1.5 kg) fresh, boned and rolled brisket
1 large onion, chopped
Water
1 meat stock cube
2 large carrots, peeled and cut into chunks
6 oz (175 g) peeled and chopped turnip

Put the brisket in a pot in which it is a fairly tight fit. Dissolve the meat cube in some hot water. Top this up with enough cold water to come halfway up the meat. Add the onion. Bring to a boil. Remove any scum which rises. Boil gently with the lid on for about 2½ hours. Remember to add the carrot and turnip about 20 mins. before your meal. The meat juices left in the pan can be strained and thickened with a little cornflour and coloured with a touch of gravy salt.

Salt Beef

Home-cooked salt beef has a wonderful flavour and I am glad to see that some butchers still offer either rolled brisket or silverside which has been brined (salted). If you want a particularly big piece for a party, you must warn your butcher at least one week (or ten days) before you intend boiling it. This is a good economical recipe and it goes a long way, especially when cold. Serve it with pickled onions and mustard. If you are serving it hot, cut in thicker slices and serve with boiled carrots and potatoes.

I remember the salting barrel in our butcher's shop. It was like a pottery dustbin!

4 lb (1.8 kg) rolled brisket (salted)
2 medium onions, peeled
4 cloves
3 medium size carrots, peeled and sliced
Small bundle parsley with a bay leaf and sprig of thyme
6 peppercorns

Steep the piece of meat in cold water for 3/4 hours. Drain and re-cover with fresh water. Stir in the two onions with the cloves stuck into them, the sliced carrots, herbs and peppercorns. Bring slowly to a boil. Lift off any scum which rises and simmer the meat for 2½ hours (30 mins to the 1 lb (½ kg) and 30 mins over). See that the lid of the pot is a good fit. To eat the meat cold press it lightly into a tight-fitting dish and set aside in the fridge.

Dundee Pies, Bridies and Fruit Tarts

PIES

Dundee bakers have always made pies in vast quantities. They were never, as far as I know, made at home. In the past minced mutton would have been the filling, but now it is minced beef. The pies are made in small straight sided ring moulds about 3 inches (7.5 cm) round, and 1½ inches (4 cm) deep. They are made so that the rim of the pastry stands up above the lid for about ½ inch (1 cm). You can buy the pies plain, or with baked beans, or mashed potato occupying the space. The pastry is very thin and made in a similar way to the hot water crust used for pork pies further south. The beauty of this pastry is that it does not readily absorb moisture, so the pies are really juicy.

BRIDIES

Forfar, just a few miles north of Dundee, is the home of the Scottish bridie, its name coming from a Miss Bridie who was said to have made the first ones. Its handy shape was quickly copied, but sadly the filling, which should be of good quality chopped steak, is very often minced like the pies. The pastry is the same, but the shape starts off like an elongated oval. The filling is placed on one side and the other side comes over to form a "D" shape. The number of round steam holes in the lid indicates with, or without, onions.

FRUIT TARTS

The non-absorbent quality of the pastry is ideal for small fruit tarts too. The bakers make them in straight sided ring moulds – a bit deeper than the pies. The fruit is usually rhubarb or apple. The juice from the fruit is thickened separately and dribbled over the top of the pies to give an appetising glaze. When I was young we lived just across the road from Wallace's bakery in Dura Street. This was long before the days of frozen fruit. Even canned fruit was rather expensive. In early Spring a board would appear outside the shop "New Season's Rhubarb Tarts," and later on in the year one for apples.

Stretchers

(or making a little go a long way)

Plenty of gravy is one of the best stretchers to make a little go a long way. Cooked dried beans added to second-day stew is another good one, and cooked pasta is another. However, a real wintertime favourite is still doughboys or suet dumplings. I know the old way was to cook the dumplings on top of the stew, but over the years I've changed to cooking them separately in a pan of boiling stock made up with a cube. At the last minute I slip them into the stew. There is less chance of the stew catching because you cannot give it a stir with all the dumplings on top.

Dried Broad Beans

Soak the beans in plenty of cold water overnight. Next day drain the beans and cover with fresh water. Bring up to a rolling boil for 10 minutes and turn the heat down to a gentle boil until the beans are cooked – just slightly firm. Drain and use as above.

Pasta

Dried macaroni shells, etc., are all cooked by the same method. Bring a large pot of salted water to the boil. Drop in the pasta, boil gently until the pasta is cooked but still fairly firm. Drain and use as above.

Parsley Doughboys

(or Suet Dumplings)

4 oz (125 g) plain flour
1½ oz (40 g) grated suet
(fresh or packet)
½ teasp. baking powder
Salt and pepper
1 tblsp. chopped parsley
Cold water
Meat stock from a cube

Mix all the dry ingredients together with enough cold water to make a soft, elastic dough. Make up the meat stock according to the packet instructions, adding more water to dilute it slightly. Dampen your hands and peel off a piece of dough about the size of a golf ball. Roll it lightly in your hands then drop it straight into the boiling stock. Turn the meat stock down to a gentle boil. Repeat with the rest of the dough. Boil for about 25/30 minutes turning the balls over once or twice. When the doughboys are cooked remove them with a slotted spoon to the hot stew and serve.

Shivery Bite

My family always fall about laughing at the name "Shivery Bite," given to the sandwich we brought with us to eat after a swim in Dundee's old shore front baths. My mother had been a keen swimmer when she was young – the opening of the Baths in the early part of the nineteen hundreds gave young women and girls their very first opportunity of a leisure sport, not to mention the slipper baths next door, where you could get a hot bath for just a few pence. The fact that there was a ladies pool and a separate men's pool is another source of hilarity for today's youngsters. I remember that there was mixed bathing on certain nights, but we thought you had to be very bold to attend then. The water was never all that warm, but there was always the hot shower in the corner. There was also a very long, narrow white sink. I'm not sure what we were supposed to use this for, but I do remember a row of us sitting in it in the hot water. The rings which overhung the deep end of the pool were great fun once you had learned to swim. Swinging from one to the other was easy, but I remember watching in awe while someone gave a marvellous display of tumbling while hanging on two rings. Our "shivery bite" was usually something in a roll. My favourite filling was fried Lorne sausage. I never did find out why the loaf shaped sausage meat was called Lorne, but it was blissfully welcome. It helped sustain us to face the blast of icy air when you left the Baths to wend your way past the Unicorn, over the narrow bridge and across and up a long road with granite sets and railway lines and out by the Royal Arch towards the tram home.

Scotch Eggs

Scotch Eggs came to mind when I was talking about the Lorne sausage. Why were Scotch Eggs so called – I have no idea? I like to buy the smallest eggs I can find for this recipe and then you will need only 3 oz (75 g) sausage meat for each egg.

12 oz (325 g) sausage meat
1 level teasp. dried thyme
4 small eggs to boil
1 small egg to use with the breadcrumbs (raw)
4 oz (125 g) dried breadcrumbs
Pepper and salt
Oil for deep frying

It is best to make Scotch Eggs on the day you intend to eat them. (Leave them overnight and they develop an ugly black ring round the yolk.) Boil the four eggs for 8-10 minutes, depending on size. When cool enough to handle peel off the shell and set aside. Now prepare the sausage meat. Put it into a bowl with the dried thyme, salt and pepper, and mix it well. Shake some dry flour over the meat and shape it into a fat sausage. Divide the sausage carefully into four pieces. Using flour on your hands flatten the sausage meat out to a circle and mould it round an egg. Take care to encase the egg with no cracks in the sausage meat. Repeat with the other three eggs. Set in the 'fridge to allow the meat to firm up. Now dip each sausage ball into beaten egg and then into the dried crumbs. Deep fry in hot oil and drain on kitchen paper.

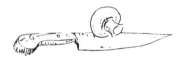

Simple Dip for Scotch Eggs

4 fluid oz thick natural yoghurt
1 level teasp. finely chopped onion
1 teasp. tomato sauce
Salt and pepper

Mix all the ingredients and season lightly. Allow to stand for 2/3 hours for flavour to develop.

CLOUTIE DUNPLING

A Cloutie Dumpling

(A Fruit Dumpling boiled in a Cloth or Cloot)

Birthday cakes were an expensive luxury when I was young in Dundee. Instead I had a large, dark, fruity dumpling which had been boiled in the wash-house boiler. I had no candles on top, but inside were silver charms and three-penny bits wrapped up in little screws of greaseproof paper. It was very exciting to unwrap the tiny wet parcel to find your charm. The disher-up had her work cut out too, making sure every child got a slice with a tell-tale paper peeping through. As girls we all wanted a ring, which meant we would not be spinsters. The cat was popular too, for good luck. We ate the dumpling in hot slices. Next day it became another pudding as thick slices were fried in butter and then sprinkled with sugar. It also turned up with bacon at breakfast – a sweet and savoury mixture which is still popular today. Most butchers and supermarkets in Scotland sell a fruit slice for this purpose.

You will need a 24 inch square of cotton from an old, clean sheet or pillowcase, and a very large pan. A jam pan will do but improvise a lid with a double thickness of wide foil so that you can tuck it over to keep in the steam.

To get the dumpling out once it is cooked have ready a large mixing bowl and ashet. Lift the cloth with strong tongs and dunk it briefly in a sink of cold water. This helps to prevent the cloth from sticking. Now sit the pudding in the bowl, untie the string, and hang the cloth over the sides. Now cover the pudding with the ashet and invert it. Remove the cloth carefully, the dumpling will be sticky. Long ago the much prized shiny, thick skin would be formed by leaving the dumpling in front of the fire, and turning it frequently. 15-20 minutes in a low oven will do the trick too.

1 lb (450 g) self raising
    white flour
1/2 lb (225 g) raisins
1/2 lb (225 g) mixed dried
    fruit
1 level teasp. bicarbonate of
    soda   .
Large pinch of salt
1 large carrot, peeled and
    grated
1 medium cooking apple,
    peeled and grated
1 small egg
2 1/2 oz (65 g) grated suet
1 large teasp. mixed spice
1 level teasp. ground ginger
1 tblsp. black treacle
A little water and charms
    (see above)

In a large mixing bowl mix the dry ingredients very thoroughly. Stir in the wrapped charms and all the other ingredients. You may need water to make a fairly stiff mixture. (In an old recipe I have you are instructed to make the dumpling stiff so that you can pick it up, shape it into a ball, and roll it in dry flour!) Have the water boiling in your large pan. Dip the cloot (or cloth) into it and wring out. Spread the damp cloth on a table and sprinkle dry flour in the centre where the dumpling is going to "sit." Turn the dumpling out. Now sprinkle more dry flour all over. Gather up the edges of the cloth and tie up the bundle, leaving some room for expansion. It is a good plan to put an old plate in the boiling water and sit the dumpling on this. The boiling water should come about 2/3 way up the dumpling. Bring to a boil, turn down the heat to a gentle boil for about three hours. If the plate stops rattling it means that the dumpling is boiling dry. Top up frequently with boiling water. See above for the method of unwrapping the dumpling and drying off the skin.

BLACK RANGE

The Irish Connection

The names in our family are nearly all Irish – Donnelly, Cosgrove, Blaney, Higgins – all descendants of the Irish immigrants who came to Dundee looking for work. March 17th, St. Patrick's Day, was a wildly exciting one for us children. There was always a huge school's concert in a jam-packed Caird Hall with music, poetry, and dance from children of all ages. We practised for weeks for this event and, when the day came, we sat row upon row on the stage facing a huge audience. When our turn came to rise and march down to the stage to do our piece we were all dressed in our Sunday best. It's a long time since I heard a whole class reciting poetry the way we used to.

Over the years many cooking traditions have melted into the Scottish way of life. Willie Low makes an excellent soda bread. Originally this would have been baked on a girdle or in a closed pot in the oven. My version, which I make almost every week, goes into the oven uncovered. However, if you like a less crusty loaf, you could cover the bread with a large cake tin. Another way of softening the crust is to wrap the bread in a clean towel whenever it comes out of the oven.

Irish Soda Bread

*1 lb (450 g) plain granary
   flour (or wholemeal)*
*8 oz (225 g) strong plain
   white flour*
1 teasp. each:
   Salt
   Bicarbone of soda
   Cream of tartar
2-3 teasp. sugar
*Just under 1 pint (600 ml)
   milk or milk and water
   mixed*

Put the Granary flour into a large bowl, sieve into it the strong white flour, salt, bicarbonate of soda, and cream of tartar. Stir in the sugar and mix well. Now using the milk, or milk and water mixture, mix to a soft dough (not too wet). I use a short-handled wooden spoon for this. Knead the dough gently in the bowl and then, very briefly, on a flour dusted wooden board until smooth. Shape the dough into a flat circle about 1½ inches (3.5 cm) deep, and score lightly across the surface with a knife to mark four quarters. The scoring does help with even distribution of heat. Bake in a moderate oven, Gas 5, 375°F, 190°C, for about 50-60 minutes. Test with a skewer. If it comes out dry the bread is done. If still sticky return the bread to the oven for an extra 10 minutes.

Chappit Tatties

(Mashed Potatoes)

This traditional recipe is so like Irish "champ" that it would be hard to say in which country it originated. The potatoes must be the floury or mealy kind, not the waxy ones. Something green and flavoursome might be added at the end, like chopped spring onions, chives or parsley.

2 lb (900 g) potatoes, peeled
and cut into chunks
10 fluid ounces (½ pint) hot
milk
Butter
Salt and pepper
Optional:
5-6 spring onions, chopped
or 1 tblsp. chopped chives
or 1 tblsp. chopped parsley
Butter

Cover the potatoes with water and simmer until soft, adding a little salt to the water. Drain off the water. Return the potato pan to the hob to dry off the retaining water. Take the pan off the heat and mash the potatoes until very smooth with the hot milk. Season to taste and stir in the chopped salad onions, chives or the parsley. Serve in a satisfying mound with a knob of butter melting on top.

Potato Scones

These flat, thin scones are lovely eaten warm and spread with butter. It is also a tradition to serve them with the breakfast bacon and eggs. Use a girdle, a heavy frying pan or an electric frying pan.

8 oz (225 g) smoothly
mashed potatoes which
are still warm
1 oz (25 g) melted butter
2 oz (50 g) plain white or
wholemeal flour
Knob of beef suet (from the
butcher)
Salt

Heat up the girdle slowly. Add the melted butter to the mashed potato with a little salt. Now work in enough flour with a fork to make a supple dough. Do not get the mixture too dry. Knead the dough lightly in the bowl then turn it out on to a floured board. Divide the mixture in two. Roll each piece out thinly to a circle and cut in four. Lightly grease the surface of the girdle with the knob of suet (this is easier to handle if you screw it up in a square of muslin). The temperature should be hot. Bake the scones for about 3 minutes on each side. I like to wait until very slight brown scorch marks appear before turning the scone over. Wrap in a clean towel to keep the scones soft until needed.

Boiled Bacon & Cabbage

In the old days I imagine the bacon and cabbage would have been boiled in the one pot. I tried it once, putting the cabbage in the pot for the last 15 minutes of cooking time, and I ended up with a very salty cabbage. Here is my newer version of the recipe.

2 lbs (900 g) streaky bacon in a piece
1½ lbs (675 g) winter cabbage cut up and hard core removed
1 oz (25 g) fresh breadcrumbs
½ oz (15 g) brown demerera sugar
8-10 cloves

Tie the bacon with white string to hold it together and soak it in cold water for 4/5 hours. Put it in a roomy pot and cover with cold water. Bring to a boil, reduce the heat, and simmer for 1 hour 40 minutes. Take the pan off the heat and leave until the bacon is cool enough to handle. Slice off the skin, leaving some fat underneath. Mix the breadcrumbs and sugar and spread on the fat, pressing it well in. Now slip the bacon under a hot grill to brown. Stud the surface with cloves and leave to go cold. To cook the cabbage take 1 pint of water out of the pot in which the bacon was cooked. Double the quantity with tap water. Boil this mixture and cook the cabbage in it. Test frequently to catch the cabbage at the right texture. Drain off the water and toss the cabbage in a lump of butter and season with pepper only. Serve at once with sliced cold bacon and a baked potato.

The Italian Connection

Ice cream parlours and chip shops were owned almost exclusively by the descendants of Italian immigrant families when I was young in Dundee. There were names like Forte, Esposito, Soave, and Baruffati. We lived almost next door to the Forte's chip shop in Dura Street, and knew how very hard they worked. My brother Jimmy and I were about the same age as their middle children, Rita and Lennie. Eliza Street was where we played, at whichever game was in favour at the time. "Catty and Batty," "Yo-yo's," "Huckaback." and "Rounders." If you were very lucky, at the end of a happy evening, on a frosty night, you might get a ½d for a bag of sizzling chips. Although we knew the Forte family quite well, I do not recall seeing any of the pasta dishes that we all enjoy so much nowadays. Perhaps pasta, in all its varied forms, was not as available as it is today. The only one I remember was macaroni, and the only dish we made with it was Macaroni Cheese. I do recall Mrs Forte dishing out a thick tomato soup which I knew did not come out of a tin. I cannot say I remember hearing the word Minestrone. The ice cream the "Tally's" made remains a very happy memory. A Sunday morning treat during a walk through Baxter's Park was a ½d cone with raspberry sauce trickled over it. It had to be a very special occasion to warrant a slider, or a squasher, or a "99"!!

Home Made Ice Cream
(Based on Meringue)

2 large eggs separated
2 oz (50 g soft brown sugar
¼ pint (150 ml) double
*   cream*

Use an electric whisk. Put the egg whites in a large bowl and whisk until very firm indeed. Sprinkle in the sugar and whisk again. In another bowl whip the double cream until firm. In yet another bowl use a fork to whisk the egg yolks. Take a large rubber spatula and fold the cream and the egg yolks into the meringue mixture as lightly as possible. Pour this mixture straight into a bowl which you can bring to the table. Cover over with foil and freeze until solid. Do not forget that home-made ice cream is very hard, so take it out of the freezer and put it into the 'fridge for at least 30 minutes before you need it.

Butterscotch Sauce for Ice Cream

2 oz (50 g) butter
5 oz (150 g) soft brown
*   sugar*
5 level tbsp. golden syrup
Small carton double cream
2/3 drops vanilla essence

In a small heavy-based pot allow the butter, sugar and syrup to melt until no grittiness is left. Do this slowly. Now cook gently for 3-4 minutes then take the pan off the heat. Sir in as much of the double cream as you wish. Stir until very smooth. Add vanilla last of all.

Brown Bread Ice Cream

Make up the ice cream as before and fold in 2 oz (50 g) fine, fresh, brown breadcrumbs and two tablespoons of Rum at the same time as the double cream, egg yolks, and egg whites are all being folded together. Freeze as before.

Macaroni Cheese

6 oz (175 g macaroni
2 oz (50 g) butter
1½ oz (40 g) plain flour
1 level teasp. dry mustard
Pepper
¾ pint (450 ml) milk
½ stock cube (chicken or
*   vegetable)*
6 oz (175 g) grated cheese
*   (Dunlop, Cheddar or*
*   Leicester)*

Cook the macaroni in fast boiling salted water for about 15 minutes, or until soft, but not sloppy. Drain and set aside. Dissolve the stock cube in a small amount of boiling water. Pour this and the cold milk into a pot. Sprinkle the dry flour and mustard over the top. Now use a whisk to disperse all the dry flour. Put the pan on the heat and, using a wooden spoon, stir the sauce until it thickens. Add the butter and season with pepper. Stir in most of the grated cheese then add the drained macaroni. Stir this well and pour into a pie dish. Scatter the rest of the cheese on top and reheat in a moderate oven (Gas 5, 375°F, 190°C) for about 15 minutes.

Minestrone

(A thick soup)

1 oz (25 g) bacon fat or
  butter
3 oz (75 g) streaky bacon,
  de-rinded and chopped
8 oz (225 g) onion, peeled
  and chopped
1 large stalk celery, chopped
  small
2 oz (50 g) turnip, peeled
  and diced
2 oz (50 g) carrot, peeled
  and diced
4 oz (125 g) potato, peeled
  and diced
2½ pints (1.5 litres) chicken
  stock (cubes)
2 large tblsp. tomato puree
1½ oz (40 g) dried small
  pasta shells
1 teasp. sugar
6 oz (175 g) cabbage
Peper and salt
To serve:
  Grated Parmesan cheese

Melt the fat or butter in a large pot and fry the bacon bits and chopped onion for 2 minutes. Add the celery, turnip, carrots and potato and fry for another 3 minutes, stirring all the time. Whisk the tomato puree into the stock. Then stir that into the frying vegetables along with the dried pasta. Cover the pot and simmer for about 30 minutes. Stir in the sugar and chopped cabbage. Continue cooking for another 15 minutes. Adjust the seasoning and serve in bowls with a spoonful of dried Parmesan cheese scattered on top of each bowl.

Black Bun

The origin of this very traditional Scottish cake is said to have been a bread dough with dried fruit worked into it. Nowadays a short crust pastry is used for lining the cake tin. In many ways this cake is easier to bake than a Christmas cake. It is much less likely to get scorched with too long baking. Black Bun was always in our house for our first-footers on Hogmanay.

10 oz (275 g) short crust
  pastry
2 oz (50 g) whole almonds,
  peeled and finely chopped
12 oz (325 g) currants
4 oz (125 g) raisins, chopped
2 oz (50 g) preserved orange
  peel, finely chopped
1 oz (25 g) dark soft brown
  sugar
Grated rind of one lemon
1 teasp. ground ginger
1 teasp. ground allspice
½ teasp. bicarbonate of
  soda
4 oz (125 g) butter, melted
2 medium eggs, beaten
2 tblsp. whisky

Roll out two thirds of the pastry to a large circle about 14 inches (35 cm) across and line the base and sides of a round 8 inch tin (20 cm) which has been well greased. Do not trim the edges. Try not to stretch the pastry and avoid too many folds. Press the pastry firmly into the angle at the bottom of the tin. In a large mixing bowl stir together the almonds, currants, raisins, peel, sugar, lemon rind, spices and bicarbonate of soda. Stir in the melted butter. Reserve a couple of teaspoons of the beaten eggs and stir the remainder into the mixture. Finally stir in the whisky and mix well. Pack this fruity mixture into the pastry lined tin. Take care not to tear the pastry. Level the fruit mixture. Now fold over the top of the lining pastry on to the fruit mixture. Trim this neatly to a 1 inch (2.5 cm) border. Use scissors to make a neat job of it. Now roll out the remaining pastry to make a lid. Lay the cake tin lightly on the pastry and mark its size. Cut out the circle. Wet the pastry round the top of the fruit mixture and position the pastry lid on top. Seal the edges firmly. If you are artistic roll out the remaining pastry and cut a thistle and some leaves. Before laying the decoration on the pastry top mix a little milk into the reserved beaten egg. Using a pastry brush paint this mixture all over. Now position the decoration and paint that over as well. Now, using a sharp fork or skewer, prick the pastry lid all over in a decorative pattern. This will let the steam out during baking. To bake the Black Bun line a baking sheet with a sheet of cardboard and set the tin on this. Surround the tin with a thick paper collar of three layers of brown paper. See that the collar rises above the rim of the tin. (Both these things are to protect the bun during baking.) Set the oven to Gas 3, 325°F, 160°C, and bake the bun for two hours. If the pastry top becomes brown, protect it with some crumpled greaseproof paper laid over it. Allow the bun to cool in the tin then turn out.

Shortbread

While shortbread is always associated with Scotland, the word short is used in most English speaking countries to denote something crisp and crumbly. The flat round "cake" of shortbread is a favourite gift at Christmas and Hogmanay. Dundee bakers make lovely shortbread shaped in traditional moulds, but there has always been a strong tradition of home baked shortbread too. When I did a Scottish bakery programme on I.T.V.'s Farmhouse Kitchen I borrowed several very old and beautiful wooden moulds from Kathleen Moore (Gutowski). Her old ones seem to be more deeply carved than many of the modern ones. The favourite centre decoration is a thistle. If the pattern on your cake of shortbread almost vanishes during baking it could mean that your pattern is not deep enough or that your mixture is too soft.

The old way of making shortbread is to put all the ingredients on a table or in a bowl and work them together with your hands. This way is not so good if you have hot hands. I now use a large electric mixer with a K. beater. I start off the night before by leaving the butter out of the 'fridge to soften. It must not, however, be melted. Traditionally shortbread should be anything from ½ inch (1 cm) to 1" (2.5 cm) thick.

Basic Shortbread Mixture

8 oz (225 g) unsalted or slightly salted butter (softish)
12 oz (325 g) plain white flour
4 oz (125 g) castor sugar
Extra castor sugar for sprinkling on plain cake only

SHORT BREAD USING A MOULD.

Traditional Cake of Shortbread

(Using a Mould)

First shake dry flour over the mould and then knock it on its side to remove the excess. Now warm the K. beater and the mixing bowl in very hot water and dry thoroughly. Slice the butter into the hot bowl and add all the other ingredients. Mix at about half of full speed until the mixture starts to look like damp breadcrumbs. If the bowl is warm enough the mixture might start to cling together. If not, stop the machine and, using one hand, work the crumbs together. The texture should be like soft marzipan. Take about half of the dough and knead it very lightly into a ball on a lightly floured surface. Press and roll the dough into the mould. Trim off the surplus for biscuits. Do not press too heavily with the rolling pin. Using the underside of a metal baking sheet, grease it lightly. By using the underside, the cake will slide off more easily when cooked. Lay a sheet of non-stick baking paper over the greased tin.

The next bit is sometimes difficult, getting the shaped dough out of the wooden mould. If you are using a flexible plastic mould it is an easier job. Invert your lined baking sheet over the mould. Swiftly, with your hands holding the mould and tin together, turn them upside down. If the patterned mould of dough has dropped out first time – three cheers for you! If not, try another method. Stand the mould on its side and knock it gently as you move it round. Spread out your other hand ready to catch it if it drops suddenly. Once on the baking sheet, take a skewer or a fork and prick the centre of the shortbread all over. Do this in a decorative pattern and push the fork or skewer through to the tin. This helps to keep the shortbread from rising. Bake for about one hour at Gas mark 2, 300°F, 150°C, depending on the thickness of the cake. It should be an even gold all over. Score the cake or shortbread lightly into sections when it is still cooling down. This makes it easier to break neatly when cold. Leave the cake on the tin until it firms up and is cold. Slide off the tin and when really cold store in a tin. To prevent it breaking, store on the lid and cover with the deep part of the tin.

Traditional Cake of Shortbread
(Without a Mould)

Make up the basic mixture as before and roll it out on a surface dusted with castor sugar. Roll it to the thickness you wish then cut out a large circle using a pan lid as a cutter or a round plate as a pattern. Set aside the trimmings to be used for biscuits. Line the underside of a baking sheet as before and transfer the cake. To do this use two large fish slices or the loose bottom of a quiche tin. Decorate the cake as before by pricking all over with a metal skewer or fork. Make a decorative edge all round by nipping the dough at intervals of about 1" (2.5 cm) all round. Bake as before and dust with castor sugar as the cake comes out of the oven. Cool on the tin and mark into sections. When cold break into pieces.

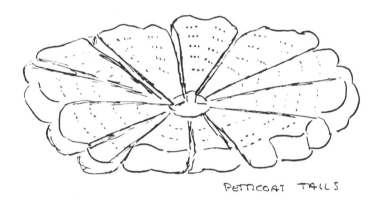

PETTICOAT TAILS

Petticoat Tails

This famous name refers to the shape of the biscuit, which is like a petticoat skirt. They are also thinner than cake shortbread. Said to have been Mary Queen of Scots favourite biscuit – maybe aye, maybe no, maybe I suppose so!

Make up the dough in the basic mixture and divide it into two pieces. Roll out the dough on a dusting of castor sugar using a pan lid or a plate to cut a circle of about 8" (20 cm) across. Transfer the circle to a baking sheet as before. Using a 2" (5 cm) biscuit cutter press into the centre of the circle. Cut the outer circle into even wedges. Prick all over each biscuit with a skewer or fork and crimp or nip the outer edge to form neat scallops. Ease each biscuit outwards so that they do not stick together and bake at the same temperature as before for about 30 minutes, or until golden. Allow to cool on the tray and when cold store in an air tight tin. Repeat with the other half of the mixture.

Shortbread Thins

This is one of the easiest ways of all to make shortbread biscuits. Nice with tea, coffee, or to accompany a light dessert. Make up the basic mixture as before and divide it into two. Dust a board with castor sugar and shape the dough into two very fat sausages. Roll to get a smooth shape, then set the pieces in the 'fridge to firm up. Do not leave until rock hard. Using a sharp, thin-bladed knife, cut really fine slices of shortbread dough and lay on a non-stick paper-lined baking sheet. Do not lay close together. Bake at the same temperature as before for about 25/30 minutes. These biscuits do not need to be pricked. They will not be perfect circles but the texture should be crisp and light. Another point – if the thin slices are slightly curled do not try to flatten them. The heat of the oven will do that. Cool and store as before.

Non-traditional variations:
The shortbread thins can be flavoured with one teaspoon of very finely chopped rosemary or one level teaspoon of crushed caraway seeds.

Shortbread Toffee Bars

There is a tin of Nestle's milk in this recipe and seeing its familiar label always reminds me of the paper carrier bag of goodies we children were each given prior to our evacuation at the start of the last war. There we were, crowds of us assembled at our school, St. Patrick's, waiting to go two by two in a long crocodile down to the station. It was quite an adventure for us, and since my mother was coming with my brother and me, we were not unduly upset. Each child was labelled like a parcel and despatched in alphabetical order – the Donnelly's, Duffy's, Donoghue's. We were sent to Montrose – a strange choice, since the aerodrome there would be just as much of a target as the Tay Bridge was thought to be!

Shortbread ingredients:
4 oz (125 g) margarine
  softened
2 oz (50 g) castor sugar
5 oz (150 g) self raising
  flour

Shortbread base:
Cream the margarine and the sugar and beat in the flour. Spread this paste-like mixture into a greased swiss roll tin 11 x 7 inches (28 x 18 cm). Bake in a moderate oven (Gas 4, 350°F, 180°C) for about 20 minutes. Leave in the tin to cool down and crisp up.

Toffee:
4 oz (125 g) margarine
4 oz (125 g) castor sugar
2 tblsp. golden syrup
6.9 oz (196 g) tin of Nestle's
condensed milk (or half a
large tin)

Topping:
4 oz (125 g) plain cooking
chocolate

Toffee:
In a heavy-based pot melt the margarine, sugar, syrup and condensed milk. Allow to boil gently until it becomes toffee coloured and thick. Drop a little into ice cold water and it should stay quite fudge like – not crisp. Pour this over the shortbread base and level the surface.

Topping:
Break the chocolate into small pieces and melt it in a heatproof bowl, either in a microwave cooker or suspended over a bowl of simmering water. Spread over the toffee and leave to cool. Turn out the block and cut into small bars.

Oven and Girdle Baking

A famous Scottish cookery writer called F. Marion McNeill said that every Scotswoman was born with a rolling pin under her arm! It is surprising, in many respects, that home baking still flourishes when you think of the marvellous choice there is from local bakers. The variety they carry, especially in teabreads and bread, is wonderful. I don't remember any fancy things being made at home when I was young, but certainly pancakes, girdle scones, and gingerbread. I still have my original copy of the Dundee Homecraft Book compiled in the early 1930's by Domestic Science teachers from Dundee schools. It cost me ninepence and was published by Paul and Matthews. It came in very handy last year when I was writing a book on all kinds of baking. I had been trying to find a recipe for Coburg cakes that I could test, and had looked in dozens of cookery books, but there it was in my tattered old school book. Coburg cakes, like queen cakes, used to be baked in little tins and were displayed "bottoms up" to show the split almond on the bottom, and the currnts in the queen cakes. Nowadays not many people would like the fiddle of greasing and later washing the patti-tins. They would almost certainly use paper bun cases.

Coburg Cakes

(Makes about 18)

6 oz (175 g self raising flour
6 oz (175 g soft tub
margarine
6 oz (175 g) soft brown sugar
1½ teasp. baking powder
1 level teasp. ground
cinnamon
1 level teasp. mixed spice
3 large eggs, beaten
1½ oz (40 g) split almonds
(or flaked almonds)
Warm water
Paper baking cases

Have your baking bowl warm and sieve into it the flour, baking powder, cinnamon, and mixed spice. Add the margarine and eggs and thoroughly mix until smooth. Add a very little warm water to achieve a soft but not sloppy mixture. Spoon into the paper baking cases which you have set into the bun tins. Fill no more than 2/3 full and top with an almond. (If you wish to be traditional put the almond in the paper case and put the mixture on top. After baking, and when the cakes are cool, peel off the paper cases and serve the cakes "upside down" showing the almonds.) Bake at Gas 4, 350°F, 180°C for about 20-25 minutes.

Variation:
The mixture can also be baked in two 7 inch (8 cm) sandwich tins. When cold sandwich the two cakes with spiced buttercream.

Spiced Butter Cream

2 oz (50 g) soft margarine
4 oz (125 g) sieved icing
sugar
¼ teasp. mixed spice

Beat all the butter cream ingredients together to a soft, smooth consistency. Add a drop of milk if necessary.

Fly Cemetery

The horror of this title used to put me off these very nice, simple fruit slices. It's fine if you want to use up some custard!

8 oz (225 g) shortcrust pastry
3 oz (75 g) currants
1 oz (25 g) raisins, chopped small
2 fat pinches of cinnamon
1 oz (25 g) castor sugar
4-5 tblsp. fairly thick custard (ordinary packet variety)
½ oz (15 g) butter cut in tiny bits
A little milk
Extra castor sugar to sprinkle

Divide the pastry in two. Roll out one half to fit a shallow, greased tin 7 x 7 inches (18 x 18 cm). Roll it so the pastry comes up the sides slightly. Put the currants, raisins, cinnamon, and sugar into a bowl and mix with enough custard to make a sticky mixture. Spread this evenly on the pastry and dot with the butter. Roll out the remaining pastry to fit the square exactly. Moisten the joining edges with water and use a fork to seal the edges all round. Score the pastry very lightly, brush with milk, and sprinkle with sugar. Bake for 20-25 minutes. Cool in tin and then transfer to a wire rack. Cut into nine squares when cold.

Black Treacle Girdle Scones

8 oz self raising white flour
Pinch of salt
¼ teasp. each ground cinnamon, ginger, mixed spice
1 large tblsp. black treacle, slightly warmed
1 small egg, beaten
A little milk

Set the girdle or frying pan over a low heat to warm up slowly. The temperature should be a little hotter than for pancakes. Sieve the flour, salt, and spices into a roomy bowl. Make a well in the centre and pour in the warm treacle. Beat the egg with a little milk, pour this on to the treacle. Now work up a soft dough, adding more milk as required. Knead the dough lightly in the bowl then turn it out on to a floured board. Divide the mixture into two pieces. Pat and roll out the dough to fit the ungreased girdle. It should be just over ¼ inch (.5 cm) thick. Turn up the heat a little and cook for about 4-5 minutes on each side. Cool in a cloth on a wire tray. Repeat with the second girdle scone.

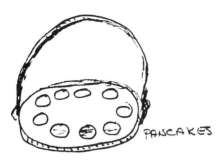

Girdle Pancakes

Use a good heavy girdle if you have one. A heavy frying pan is not bad, or even a non-stick frying pan. On the T.V. programme we often used an electric frying pan. The heat was very steady, which is what you need for pancakes. Whatever you are using heat it up slowly until it is comfortably hot. This means you can hold your open hand over it easily – a moderate heat.

8 oz (225 g) plain white flour
½ teasp. bicarbonate of soda
1 teasp. cream of tartar
1 pinch of salt
1 tblsp. castor sugar
1 large egg, beaten
About ½ pint (300 ml) milk
1 large teasp. golden syrup
Knob of suet – piece of
    muslin or cloth

Put the girdle or frying pan on a low heat. Sift the flour, salt, bicarbonate of soda, and cream of tartar, into a roomy mixing bowl. Stir in the sugar. Beat the egg, milk, and syrup into the dry ingredients until you have a thick but pouring batter. Tie up the suet in a little bundle with the muslin or cloth, and use this to put a thin film of fat on the girdle or pan by running it lightly over. Test the temperature of your girdle with just one pancake. Pour on one dessertspoon of batter from the end of the spoon. When bubbles appear on the surface flip the pancake over to cook the other side. If the girdle is too hot the underside of the pancake will burn before the bubbles burst. If too cold the bubbles will burst and the underside will still be pale. Cool the pancakes on a clean dish cloth set on a wire tray. This keeps them moist. Eat on the day they are made or freeze for future use.

Plain Girdle Scones

Neither self raising flour nor the use of an egg is traditional, but I find this mixture works well.

8 oz (225 g) self raising white
   flour
½ teasp. salt
1 teasp. sugar
1 small egg, beaten
A little milk

Set the girdle or frying pan over a low heat to warm up slowly. The temperature should be hotter than for pancakes. Sieve the flour and salt and stir in the sugar. Using the beaten egg, as well as a little milk, mix to a soft elastic dough. Divide into two pieces. Pat and roll the dough to fit the girdle – it should be just over ¼ inch thick. Cook for 5-7 minutes on each side. At the first sign of scorching turn the heat down. There is no need to grease the girdle. Cook the second scone the same way.

Snowballs

The raspberry jam in these cakes is my idea. I am fairly sure they had no colour inside and were probably sandwiched with buttercream.

4 oz (125 g) self raising
   white flour
1 teasp. baking powder
4 oz (125 g) castor sugar
4 oz (125 g) tub margarine
   (soft)
2 medium eggs, beaten
1 tblsp. warm water
2/3 drops vanilla essence

Filling and covering:
2 heaped tblsp. raspberry
   jam
8 oz (225 g) sifted icing
   sugar
A little warm water
4 oz (125 g) desiccated
   coarse coconut

Grease about fourteen round-bottomed bun tins. Sift the flour and baking powder into a bowl. Beat in the remaining ingredients until you have a soft, fairly smooth, mixture. Add a little warm water if you need to. Half fill the tins with the sponge mixture and bake for about 15-20 mins. at Gas 4, 350°F, 180°C. Leave to firm up for about five mins. Turn out carefully, using a knife to ease round the sides. When cold spread a little jam on the top of half of the buns. (If the buns are not flat, slice off a bit on top.) Cover each one with another bun to get a roundish shape. Make a runny icing with the icing sugar and a very little water. Put the coconut in a flat bowl. Stick a fork in the top of each bun and paint the bun all over with the icing then dunk in the coconut so it is coated all over. Set aside to dry.

Pavee Stanes

(Pavement Stones)

These oblong spiced biscuits are coated with royal icing which dries very hard. My granny used to send me for them to a bakers shop at the top of the Hilltown. I suspect she had to dunk them in her tea to soften them!

8 oz (225 g) plain white flour
1 teasp. baking powder
4 oz (125 g) margarine (block)
3 oz (75 g) castor sugar
1 teasp. mixed spice
2 fat pinches powdered cinnamon
1 egg, beaten
A little milk

Royal Icing:
2 teasp. egg white
3 oz (75 g) sieved icing sugar

Sift the flour, baking powder and spices into a bowl. Stir in the sugar and then rub in the margarine as if you were making pastry. Bind this mixture together with the egg. Add a drop of milk if you need to get a softish mixture. Use extra flour to roll into a long sausage and divide into about 20 pieces. Take each piece and work into a ball then into an oblong sausage. Place the biscuits on baking sheets lined with non-stick paper. Bake at Gas 6, 400°F, 200°C for about 20 mins. Allow to cool and crisp up. Ice roughly with royal icing.

Beat together until smooth.

Dundee Cake.

Dundee Cake

Dundee is probably unique in having two world-famous food specialities named after it – Dundee Cake and Dundee Marmalade. My version of Dundee Cake is lightly fruited without peel. However, one of Dundee's master bakers tells me he uses peel because Mrs Keiller, of Marmalade fame, was said to have done so to use up the peel left over from her famous preserve. The most distinctive feature of the cake is the blanched split almonds, laid in circles on the surface. The nuts are toasted brown while the cake is baking. When the cake has cooled overnight wrap it in foil or place it in a tin for two/three days to mellow. I prefer to cut in slices rather than in wedges.

6 oz (175 g) soft butter or
tub margarine
4 oz (125 g) soft brown
sugar
½ teasp. almond essence
7 oz (190 g) plain white
flour
1 level teasp. baking powder
6 oz (175 g) currants
6 oz (175 g) sultanas
2 oz (50 g) red glacé cherries,
chopped small
3 large eggs
1½ oz (40 g) whole or split
blanched almonds
1 oz (25 g) ground almonds

Grease an 8 inch (20 cm) round baking tin and put a circle of greaseproof paper in the bottom. In a medium sized bowl cream together the butter (or margarine), sugar and almond essence. Into another bowl sift the flour and baking powder. Into this mix all the prepared fruit and ground almonds. In a third bowl beat the eggs. Fold the eggs a little at a time, and fruit likewise, into the creamed mixture. Do not beat. I use a strong spatula. Mix well. Turn cake mixture into the tin. Level the surface. Lay the blanched almonds in circles. Bake the cake in a warm oven, Gas 3, 325°F, 160°C for 45 minutes. Turn down the heat to Gas 1, 275°F, 140°C for about one hour longer. Check that the cake is cooked by the skewer method. If it is sticky, bake a little longer.

N.B. To protect the cake during baking I place a sheet of cardboard on the baking sheet and then put the cake on top. A further protection is a collar of three layers of brown paper to surround the outside of the tin, and standing above the rim of the tin. Make the collar by stapling the layers together. (The collar can be used over and over again.)

Sweeties

The Scots have a sweet tooth and Dundonians are no exception. Sweeties, and in particular the hard-boiled kind, stay in my mind as much for the coloured stripes as for their various flavours. My brother Jimmy and I vied with each other to be the one to pay the weekly bill at our corner shop. A free "poke" (paper bag) of "bilings" (hard-boiled sweets) was our reward from Mrs Rose, the shop owner. They were sold loose from a big glass jar and had various flavours like lemon, raspberry, aniseed, and horehound. Sherbet dabs, soor plooms, striped bas, snowballs and sugerelly straps – the list was endless and a difficult decision with your Saturday "make" (halfpenny). The big brass scales clanked into life with your small purchase and another quick flick turned a flat square of paper into a "poke." Halloween was a favourite time for sweet making at home with cinder toffee and "kelly" (sherbet).

Cinder Toffee

This is sometimes called sponge candy because the bicarbonate of soda makes it froth up to look like a sponge with holes in it.

*2 lbs (900 g) brown or white
 sugar
6 fluid ozs (175 ml) cold
 water
2 level teasp. bicarbonate of
 soda
(Watch out for lumps –
 sieve it if you have to)*

Put the sugar and water in a very large pan with a heavy base over a medium heat until the sugar has dissolved. Turn up the heat to a steady boil for about 20 minutes, or until the hard crack stage. This is when a few drops of the syrup, when poured into a cup of cold water, sets immediately – often in long threads. These threads should snap easily – rather than bend. Take the pan off the heat and immediately add the bicarbonate of soda. The toffee will froth up in an alarming way – stir it and quickly pour into a well-greased tin – a deep roasting tin is ideal. Mark into large squares before it goes cold. It should break easily.

Toffee Apples

Wooden sticks are not easy to find, since butchers no longer use them. I use flat lolly sticks. They are rather small so I tend to use very small apples.

12 small, perfect, sweet
apples and 12 sticks
1 lb (450 g) white sugar
2 oz (50 g) butter
1 tblsp. golden syrup
2 teasp. vinegar
¼ pint (150 ml) water

Wipe and dry the apples and push a stick into each stalk end. Put all the ingredients into a large heavy-based pan over a gentle heat until the sugar has dissolved. Turn up the heat to a steady boil. Allow the syrup to come to the hard crack stage as described in the cinder toffee recipe. Remove the pan from the heat and tilt it to one side. Carefully dip each apple into the toffee. Twirl it round to get an even coating, then tap the handle gently on the side of the pan before setting it down on a very well greased baking tin. If the toffee sets too quickly put the pan back over a gentle heat. Another method is to put the pan of toffee straight into a bowl of boiling water to achieve the same effect.

Treacle Toffee

8 oz (225 g) black treacle
8 oz (225 g) sugar
4 oz (125 g) butter
2 teasp. vinegar

Put all the ingredients together into a large heavy-based pan and bring to a gentle boil. Check that the sugar has dissolved. Continue boiling for about 20 minutes, or until the syrup reaches the hard crack stage as described in the cinder toffee recipe. Pour into a well greased shallow tin. Mark into small squares before the toffee sets hard. Break into pieces and wrap each piece in waxed paper or use the inner lining of a cornflakes packet.

N.B. Hard crack will be marked on a sugar boiling thermometer as 265°F, 130°C. Also, when making any sort of toffee it should not be stirred too often once the sugar has dissolved.

Sherbet

(A modern version)

Sherbet Dabs are still sold in the distinctive yellow paper tubes. There was a choice of licking stick. This could be either liquorice or a tiny lollipop on a wooden stick.

1½ teasp. bicarbonate of soda
2 teasp. citric acid powder
6 teasp. castor sugar
4 teasp. instant lemon mousse powder

Shake all the ingredients through a sieve and into a bowl. Pack into tiny glass jars with a stick of "sugarellie."

Tablet

(Slightly harder than fudge)

I associate tablet with sales of work and church bazaars. There was always a square biscuit tin in the porch of our church full of neatly-wrapped bars of tablet. Some energetic person must have made it every week to help church funds. The recipe can be varied with the addition of chopped nuts or glacé cherries, but the true, buttery, creamy delight, to my mind, needs no embellishments.

2 lbs (900 g) granulated sugar
7½ fluid ozs (200 ml) fresh milk
2 oz butter
1 small tin condensed milk (7 oz/190 g)
¼ teasp. vanilla essence

Use a large, heavy-based pan if possible. Put sugar, milk and butter in it over a low heat and stir until the sugar is dissolved. Bring to a boil. Take the pan off heat and stir in condensed milk. Return pan to the heat and boil gently (stirring occasionally) until the soft ball stage. This is marked on a sugar thermometer 240°F, 116°C. To test for soft ball have a small jug of ice cold water, dip a teaspoon in the hot mixture and drop some into the iced water. You should be able to pick up the sugar balls and roll them between your fingers. Remove the pan from the heat and allow to settle. Stir in the vanilla essence. Use a wooden spoon to beat the mixture until it starts to "grain" and feel stiffish. Pour immediately into an oiled Swiss roll tin 7" x 11" (18 x 28 cms). When nearly cold mark into bars. When cold snap the bars apart and wrap.

Coconut Ice

This was another bazaar favourite. Look for coarsely grated coconut. It does give a better flavour. However, the finer packet coconut makes it easier to cut into neat fingers. My rougher coconut comes from a health food shop. Be sure to ask for grated or desiccated coconut. The flaked and stranded coconut is sometimes sweetened.

1 lb (450 g) granulated sugar
¼ pint (150 ml) water
4 oz (125 g) dessicated coconut
Margarine or butter to grease a small swiss roll tin 11" x 7" (27 x 18 cm).
Pink colouring (optional)

Put the sugar and water in a large pan, preferably a heavy-based one. Heat gently until the sugar dissolves. Bring to a gentle boil and allow to boil without stirring until a drop of mixture forms into a soft ball in a jug of cold water. You should be able to pick it up and roll it in your fingers. This time is very variable depending on your size of pan – about 3/5 minutes. Remove pan from heat. Stir in the pink colour if you wish – 2/3 drops. Add the coconut and stir and beat until the mixture grains – that is gets sugary round the edges. Scrape this down from the sides and continue beating until the mixture is thick. Pour quickly into tin and level. Mark into bars when cool and break into bars when cold. Wrap in greaseproof or cellophane paper.

Butterscotch

I used to call soft brown sugar "Scotch pieces of sugar" and we could buy it at the corner grocer for ½d a bag. You ate it with the help of a wet finger.

1 lb (450 g) soft brown sugar
4 oz (125 g) unsalted butter
10 fluid ozs (½ pint) milk

Take a heavy-based, roomy pot and put all three ingredients in it. Start over a low heat until all the sugar melts and there is no grittiness left. Boil at a higher heat to the hard crack stage. To test this dribble one teaspoon of the mixture into a jug of ice cold water. When it sets on its way down in long, crisp strands which snap when you touch them pour the butterscotch into a well-greased Swiss roll tin. Mark into squares when still warm and break into pieces when cold.

Raspberries

I think I was nine when I went to the berries. It wasn't really proper berry-picking because it was just at a small holding at the east side of Baxter's Park. Two or three of us had heard you could earn a bit of pocket money. We were lucky, the old boy took us on at ½d per punnet! I can hear him yet, shouting down the rows at us "Pick clean lassies, pick clean." I daresay we were not too careful about searching under the canopy of leaves for the ripe fruit. The fruit season came and went very swiftly. It was a risky business waiting for the price of berries to come down – if you waited too long there was no raspberry jam for a year. We had no freezers then for storing our precious fruit.

Scottish raspberries have a special quality which make them extra good for jam. Perhaps it is the longer maturing time in the cool climate. If we are lucky enough to catch the season we often stop at Inchture to buy a trayful of berries to pack and freeze away the minute we get home. Because of all the food I make in rehearsal, and what I bring ready-made for my opening display on my programme, I have three huge freezers.

Raspberry Jam

The smell of jam cooking is wonderful and while I cannot claim it is cheaper to make your own, it certainly has a better flavour. The best time to make jam is immediately the berries are picked. This is not always easy to time, but fruit which has to sit overnight, or which has come out of the freezer, loses part of its pectin. This is the ingredient which is crucial to setting.

5 lbs (2.25 g) fresh raspberries (add an extra 1 lb (450 g) if you use frozen or very soft fruit
5 lbs (2.25 g) granulated sugar

Use a large, heavy pot. Pick over the fruit carefully and discard any plugs still left in the berries (green stalk and white centre). Do not wash or rinse unless you absolutely have to. Put the fruit in a pot over a low heat and, using a potato masher, break down the fruit to produce plenty of juice. Once this is done turn up the heat just a bit to bring the fruit to simmering point. The idea is to allow the juices to evaporate slowly. Do not add sugar until the fruit is a thick pulp. It is important to keep stirring as the pulp gets thicker and thicker. Meanwhile, wash five jars and screw-top lids and pop the jars in a warm oven along with the sugar. You can leave the sugar in bags or turn it all out into a shallow, wide dish. Warming the sugar helps speed up the boiling process. Stir in the sugar and, once it has all melted, turn up the heat and boil to setting point. This is when a teaspoon of jam wrinkles on a cold saucer after it has cooled down, and you push it gently. Pour into the jars and seal at once with the screw tops. Store in a dark cool place.

Fresh Raspberry Sauce

(For Ice Cream)

4 oz (125 g) fresh raspberries
1 oz (35 g castor sugar

Put the berries into a small, heavy pot and break them up with a fork. Stir in the sugar and cook gently until the sugar dissolves. You can serve the sauce as it is but if you want to get rid of the seeds you must strain through a piece of muslin, lining a nylon sieve.

CRANACHAN

Cranachan

I do not know where this recipe originated, but it is a good way of showing off three high quality products – oatmeal, fresh raspberries and rich cream. I think it looks its best in tall, thin glasses. You will need six.

6 oz (175 g) medium oatmeal
1 lb (450 g) perfect
*   raspberries*
2 oz (50 g) castor sugar
10 fluid ozs double cream

Set aside six perfect raspberries. First shake the oatmeal over a largish baking sheet and toast the oatmeal, either in the oven or under the grill. Watch it carefully, it burns easily. Leave the oatmeal to cool. Now check over the raspberries and crush them a little to bring out some juices. Sweeten the cream with the sugar and whip it until at the floppy stage, but not stiff. Assemble in the glasses at the last minute to keep the oatmeal crisp. Layer the fruit, cream, oats and finish with a layer of cream. Perch a raspberry on top of each glassful and serve cool.

Hot Toddy and Highland Coffee

Both these recipes may well be considered worse than treason by the whisky connoisseur. However, there is something very comforting about a powerful drink like whisky tempered with sugar or honey or cream and coffee. The quantities must be vague, so add sweetening and liquor in the proportion which suits you. I shall just give you the general method.

Hot Toddy

Warm your glass by half filling it with hot water. Let it stand until the glass is very hot. Pour away the water. Put sugar in the glass and pour in more hot water. Stir the sugar round and when it has melted add your whisky. Lemon juice is another popular addition at this point and you can also substitute honey for the sugar.

Highland Coffee

Again heat your glass by the same method as above. Pour the water away and add sugar to taste. Pour in freshly-made hot coffee and stir until the sugar dissolves. Add your whisky and, to add a final, glorious touch, float about ¼ inch of double cream over the surface of the Highland Coffee. Do not stir in the cream, but drink the whisky-sweetened coffee through the layer of double cream. You may need a spoon to rescue the last of the cream from the bottom of the glass.

Dundee Marmalade

The sharp tang of Seville oranges is unmistakable. They make the very best marmalade. The story goes that a young Dundee grocer, James Keiller, rashly bought up a cheap consignment of the bitter oranges that had arrived at the port. It would be nice to think that he did not realise they were bitter, and that his hard working, thrifty wife Janet saved the day by turning them into the orange preserve which became popular in his shop. The date was 1700. Several years later, in 1797, another Mrs Keiller and her son, James, started off the world's first marmalade factory. Today more than half a million pounds of marmalade are eaten every day. When I was young, and by then Keiller's made not only marmalade but jams and sweeties, it was often possible to identify what was being made because of the smell floating round the town – quite near to Samuel's clock. I can recall the horse drawn carts loaded with wooden barrels of pulp from the fruit fields of the Carse of Gowrie driving up the Pend to Keiller's. Marmalade is also made from lemons, tangerines, grapefruit and umpteen other variations. This recipe is straight-forward Seville orange marmalade which I have made in vast quantities all my life. I now use a food processor for speed and this gives a nice chunky texture. For perfect peel you must return to cutting the peel by hand in narrow strips.

Dundee Seville Orange Marmalade

Timings are not easy to give, since a very large jam pan with a shallow depth of fruit will cook more quickly than a smaller pan and a deeper volume of fruit.

MAKES 10 POTS

3 lbs (1.3 Kg) Seville oranges
  (fresh)
2 whole lemons
6 lbs (2.7 Kg) granulated
  sugar
6 pints water

Pour boiling water over the oranges and the lemons. Leave until cool enough to handle. Squeeze the juice from the two lemons and discard the skins. Put the juice into a large jam pan or a large, heavy-based pan. I use a 14 pint aluminium pan. Perhaps, of course, I should say pot. In Scotland pots are pans in which you cook. In England pots are dishes on which you put your food!! Cut the oranges in two and, using an ordinary lemon squeezer, get out most of the juice and pour it into the jam pan. Put all the seeds in another bowl. Search through each orange shell for more seeds. Cut each shell in three pieces. Now, in 2/3 batches, reduce the orange peel in a food processor until it is chunky. Watch it carefully. Tip all the chopped peel into the pan with the lemon and orange juice and add six pints of water. Pips are very necessary to get a good set, so tie them up with string in muslin or a piece of fine nylon curtain net. Make a tight "Dick Whittington" bundle, and drop this into the pan as well. Cover the pan and leave overnight or for about six hours. This softens the peel.

Next day bring the contents of the pan up to a boil, turn down the heat and allow to boil gently, uncovered, so that the liquid will evaporate. Allow this mixture to cook until it is just a thick mush. Stir often to prevent sticking. Meanwhile warm the sugar in a low oven (or for ½ minute in the microwave – you can leave it in its paper bags). Stir the sugar into the fruit until it dissolves. Turn up the heat again and boil the marmalade until setting point. Watch out, it will spit – that's why you need a big pan. Test for setting point in about 15/20 minutes, but it may take much longer. Put one teaspoon of marmalade on a cold saucer and put it in the 'fridge. After one minute if, when you push the marmalade sideways, it forms a skin, then the heat can be turned off. I lift my pan onto a wooden board and stir in a knob or two of butter to disperse the foam. Don't be in too much of a hurry, if you pot your preserve immediately the fruit will all float up to the top. Use warm jars (from the oven) and screw on the metal twist tops immediately, or cover the surface of the marmalade with a wax disc. Cover the cellophane when cold. The screw tops are much better if you can get them, or re-use old ones which are in perfect condition. Store in a dark, dry cupboard.

N.B. The old brass jam pans, which everybody used when I was young, are now frowned on. Use them decoratively for plants and polish frequently!

Seville oranges come into the shops in January and February. The season is short, so freeze oranges whole to make your preserve later on. Just scrub the oranges, dry and pop into plastic bags. When using frozen fruit add two or three extra oranges to the amount in the recipe. The ability to set diminishes in the freezer and the extra oranges help.

GRACE'S
T.V.
RECIPES

GRACE'S T.V. RECIPES

Cucumber Soup

3 large cucumbers
1 lb (450 g) onions, peeled
    and chopped
2 pints chicken stock (cubes)
1 glass sherry
Salt
5 fl oz (¼ pint) single cream
2 oz (50 g) butter
Salt and white pepper

Peel the cucumbers and remove the seeds down the middle. The easiest way to do this is to split the cucumber lengthways and use a teaspoon to scrape down the centre. Cook the onions with the butter in a big pot until they are soft. Chop the cucumbers and add to the onion. Pour in the sherry, cook gently for about 10 mins. Keep shaking the pan so that nothing sticks. Pour in the stock, season with salt and pepper and continue cooking until the cucumber is soft. Strain off the liquid. Put the soft vegetables through a food processor or liquidiser. Return the pulp to the pan and stir in the liquid. Taste and adjust the seasoning and pour all the soup through a sieve if you want a very smooth result. Reheat and stir in the cream just before serving.

This soup is also very good cold.

Bell Inn Smokies

A famous restaurant chef at the Bell Inn in Aston Clinton in Buckinghamshire devised this recipe. It is very good.

1 pair Arbroath smokies
2 good sized fresh tomatoes
5 fl oz (¼ pint) double
* cream*
Black pepper & salt

Use four medium size ramekins. Fillet and flake the flesh of the two smokies. Skin the tomatoes by plunging them first in boiling water and then into cold. Dice the tomato flesh, removing the seeds as you go. Put the tomato pieces in the four ramekins, season with salt and pepper, then pack the flaked fish into the ramekins. Pour a thin layer of cream in each dish. Put dishes on a baking tin and cook in a hot oven for five to six minutes until bubbling and touched light brown. Serve hot with thinly cut buttered brown bread.

Salmon Cutlets
with an Avocado Mayonnaise

1 small onion
1 small carrot
1 bay leaf
½ pint (300 ml) dry white
* white (small can)*
Salt & white pepper
4 - 8 oz (225 g) salmon
* cutlets*

Sauce:
¼ pint (150 ml) mayonnaise
1 large ripe avocado
1 tblsp. fresh lemon juice
3 tblsp. brandy (or dry
* sherry)*

Peel and slice both the onion and carrot and put into a wide, flattish pot with a lid. Stir in the wine, bay leaf, salt and pepper. Bring to a boil and simmer for 10 mins. Add the salmon cutlets, cover and simmer on a low heat for about 7/8 mins.

Sauce:
Peel and stone the avocado and slice the flesh. Put the mayonnaise, brandy, avocado and lemon juice in a food processor until smooth. Remove the salmon cutlets from the pot and set one on each plate and allow to cool. Discard the vegetables and simmer the juices left in the pot until they reduce to about two tablespoons. Stir the juices into the mayonnaise and serve with a plain, green lettuce salad and steamed new potatoes.

Tagliatelle Carbonara

1 lb (450 g) dried tagliatelle
1 medium onion, peeled &
  finely chopped
1 tblsp. oil
3 oz (75 g) chopped, cooked
  ham or grilled smoky
  bacon
3 dessertsp. grated parmesan
  cheese
4 dessertsp. tomato sauce
Olive oil or single cream

Cook the onion in the oil until it is soft. Boil the tagliatelle in plenty of water until just soft and no more. Do not overcook. Drain the pasta and return it to the warm pot. Stir in the onion, ham or bacon, cheese and tomato sauce. Add enough olive oil or single cream to coat all the pasta. Stir well, reheat with sauce and serve at once.

Honeyed Back Bacon

(To eat cold)

2 lb (900 g) back bacon in a
  piece (plain or smoked)
1 level tblsp. runny honey
1 tblsp. fresh breadcrumbs
1 teasp. lemon juice
Salt & pepper

Remove the rind from the bacon but leave a layer of fat behind. Tie bacon with white string into a neat parcel. Place in a large pot and cover with cold water. Bring to a boil, lift off any grey scum which rises and taste the water. If it is extremely salty, pour away and start again with fresh water. Simmer the meat gently for about 50 mins. and leave to cool in the water. If you are using a pressure cooker the bacon will cook in 25 mins. Switch on the grill so that it is hot when you need it. In a small bowl mix the honey, lemon, breadcrumbs and seasoning. Press the sticky mixture over the fatty top of the back bacon (having firstly removed the string). Stand the bacon on a heat-proof plate and slide it under the grill. Leave until the crumbs begin to brown. Remove from the heat and cool down. Serve sliced with salad and a baked potato, or use for delicious top quality sandwiches.

Crispy Sirloin Pieces with Garlic and Ginger

1½ lb (750 g) sirloin steak
   in a thick slice
1 small cube fresh, peeled
   ginger, finely chopped
¼ teasp. garlic, peeled and
   chopped
4 tblsp. natural yoghurt or
   double cream
1 level teasp. salt
1 large egg, beaten
Dried breadcrumbs
Oil to fry the meat cubes

Use scissors to chop the meat into one-inch cubes (remove skin and outside fat). Mix all ingredients except egg, breadcrumbs and oil. Stir the meat into the yoghurt mixture. Stir well so that the cubes are well coated. The whole lot looks a sticky mess, but leave it for at least three hours. Using two shallow dishes, put the beaten egg in one and the dried breadcrumbs in the other. Dip the cubes of meat first in the egg and then in the dried crumbs. Fry the meat pieces in a shallow pan with plenty of oil. Keep turning the cubes until brown. Check that the meat is either well-done or pink in the centre, if that is what you like. Dry the crispy meat off on kitchen paper. Serve reheated with rice and a sweet and sour sauce.

Grouse

The reddish-brown birds are easily recognised in the wild with their feathered legs and feet. They live mostly in the cold north and west of Scotland and Ireland. Their moorland diet of heather buds and wild berries probably accounts for their superb, rich and gamey flavour.

No fancy recipes are needed, but the accompaniments, and the gravy in particuar, need careful attention. My way of dealing with the high proportion of bone to meat is the one I also use for small ducks.

In some quarters there is a great race, similar to the Beaujolais rush, to have freshly shot birds on the menu on the great day.

This makes nonsense of the theory that game should be hung before cooking. My advice is to seek out a poulterer with a game licence, a rare bird himself nowadays. He will hang the birds in feather for two to four days in cold weather and less if it is warm.

They must then be plucked, wiped (not washed), drawn and made ready for cooking. The traditional accompaniments to roast grouse are game chips, a sharp jelly made from Rowan berries, fried breadcrumbs and bread sauce. Long ago the liver was lightly cooked in butter, mashed and spread on circles of toasted bread. Each bird was served sitting on a little circle of its own.

The game chips should be cooked like ordinary chips but cut very finely – about the thickness of two match sticks. You could use the crispy packet variety but they are not nearly as good. I like to serve very creamy mashed potatoes so that the contrasting crunchy breadcrumbs can be spooned over the top.

Roast Red Grouse

*One brace of young grouse
(about 1¼ to 1½ lb each
(600 to 750 g)
2 oz (50 g) butter, softened
1 level teasp. dry mustard
Salt and pepper
4 strips of fatty bacon
8 tiny onions, peeled
(overgrown salad onions
or shalots)*

Gravy:
*1½ pints water
1 medium onion, peeled
and chopped
1 small carrot, scrubbed
and chopped
1 bay leaf
Giblets
Salt and pepper
1 tblsp. cornflour
Spot of gravy browning*

Start early in the day. Remove the giblets from the birds and put in a pan with the gravy ingredients, except the cornflour and the gravy browning. Bring to a simmer and leave to cook for about 20 mins.

Back to the grouse. Wipe the birds inside and out with kitchen paper, season well. Mix the butter with the mustard and put a knob of butter and four onions inside each bird. Use the rest of the butter to spread over the breasts. Put the birds in a small roasting tin and cover with the fatty bacon. Roast uncovered in a moderate oven, gas 5, 375°F, 190°C, for 35-40 minutes, depending on the size. Remove the bacon about 10 minutes before the end of cooking time. Cut it up small and set aside. Baste often during the roasting and if there is little juice add a splash or two of water or wine to the tin.

Remove the birds and shake out the onions from the inside and any juices. Scrape the juices in the roasting tin into the gravy pan. When the birds are cool use a pair of scissors to cut through the bone on the breast and cut away all the underside so that you are left with four oval pieces of meat on a small amount of bone. Put the trimmings in the gravy pan as well and leave that to go on cooking.

Set aside the breast meat pieces in a clean roasting tin. Add the chopped bacon and small onions and cover with the foil ready for reheating.

Back to the gravy. When the stock is really full of flavour strain into another pan and pour about a cup of this stock into the roasting tin with the grouse. Use this to baste while reheating.

Thicken the rest of the stock with the cornflour and stir gently over a low heat until it thickens. Darken the colour of the gravy with browning if necessary.

Fried breadcrumbs:
2 oz (50 g) butter
1 dessertsp. oil
4 - 6 oz (125 - 175 g) fresh
  white breadcrumbs
Salt and pepper

Melt the butter and oil in a heavy frying pan. Add the crumbs, turning over continuously with an egg slice over a low heat until brown and crispy. Season well. Take time and care as the crumbs burn easily. When cold the crumbs will store well for a day or two in a tin.

Wild Rowan and Apple Jelly:
1 lb (450 g) Rowan berries
1 lb (450 g) crab apples or
  tart cooking apples
2 pints water
1 lb (450 g) preserving sugar

Strip the berries off the stalks, rinse and dry them on an old kitchen towel. Wipe the apples and chop into small pieces. Put the Rowans and the apples into a roomy pan with the water. Stew gently. Mash until everything is soft and pulpy, about 45 minutes.

Strain this through a layer of muslin lining a nylon sieve. Do not push but leave for the liquid to drip through into a bowl. You should have a pint of juice (600 ml).

Weigh out 1 lb (150 g) sugar per pint of juice. Heat the juice in a clean, roomy pan. Add the sugar and stir over a low heat until the sugar has completely dissolved. Bring to a gentle boil and boil until setting point is reached. Pot into small jars and cover in the usual way.

Bread Sauce:
1 medium onion, peeled and
  pierced with three whole
  cloves
¾ pint (450 ml) milk
¼ teasp. salt
6 black peppercorns
Small piece of bay leaf
6 - 8 oz (175 - 225 g) fresh
  breadcrumbs
½ oz (15 g) butter

Put the onion in a saucepan with the milk, salt, peppercorns and bay leaf. Cover and place over a low heat and bring almost to the boil. Set aside and leave for 30 minutes at least. Strain the flavoured milk into a bowl. Add the breadcrumbs, butter and stir well, this should be a thick mixture. Place in the oven, covered, and heat for about 20 minutes.

Chocolate and Maraschino Gateau

You could say that this is my version of the famous Black Forest Gateau. I use a fatless chocolate sponge base which I much prefer to cake. The cherries are the kind you buy to put in cocktails and have a maraschino flavour. Their firm texture contrasts beautifully with the soft texture of the gateau. Look for a jar of red cherries in a clear pinkish rather than dark red liquid. They are both fine but the dark red syrup makes the cream go a funny colour, although the taste is unaltered. If you can get the maraschino liqueur with which to soak the sponge, so much the better. If not, use a good sherry.

SERVES 12

Fatless Chocolate Sponge
3 large eggs
3 oz (75 g) castor sugar
2 teasp. cocoa powder, sifted
(not drinking chocolate)
3 oz (75 g) plain white flour

Grease and base line an 8 inch (20 cm) cake tin with sides about 3 inches (75 cm) deep. Preheat the oven to moderate, Gas 3, 325°F, 160°C.

Using an electric mixer or an electric hand whisk, whip the eggs and sugar until they have increased in volume and are very, very thick and fluffy.

Mix the cocoa powder and flour and, using a sieve, shake about one-third of the flour mixture over the whipped eggs and sugar. Fold this in carefully, using a spatula and a figure of eight movement, sliding the spatula to the bottom of the bowl so that no dry flour is left. Repeat this twice, taking care to cut through the mixture with the sharp edge of the spatula to keep the mixture as fluffy as possible.

Pour this mixture into the tin and bake for about 40 mins., or until the sponge is risen, firm to the touch and beginning to shrink from the sides of the tin.

Leave in the tin for about 10 mins., then slide a knife carefully round the sponge and turn it out onto your open hand. Peel off the lining paper and turn the sponge over again and onto a wire try to cool. The sponge sometimes sinks in the centre.

Filling and Covering:
4 fl oz (125 ml) maraschino
liqueur or sherry
4 fl oz (125 ml) water

To fill the gateau, select a large serving plate, as flat as possible. Slice the cold sponge horizontally into three layers and place the bottom slice on the serving plate.

4 fl oz (125 ml) syrup from
    cherries
½ pint (300 ml) double
    cream
1 single portion carton of
    chocolate mousse (about
    2 - 3 tblsp.)
8 oz jar (225 g) maraschino-
    flavoured red cherries in
    syrup, drained and cut in
    half

**Chocolate Caraque to
decorate:**
2 oz (50 g) best quality plain
    chocolate, broken into
    small   pieces
1 little salad oil
Extra whipped cream
    (optional)

In a jug, mix the liqueur, water and syrup and pour about one-third of this mixture over the sponge on the plate. Stop pouring before the liquid starts oozing out of the sponge.

Whip the cream to the floppy stage and spread two generous tablespoons on the sponge. Do this carefully as the sponge will be very soft. Spread about half the chocolate mousse on top of the cream, and top this with half the cherries.

Put the middle slice of sponge in position and repeat the layers of liquid, cream and mousse, and top with the remaining cherries.

Put the top layer of sponge on and pour over the remaining liquid (you may have to add a little extra at this point). Press the sponge down carefully.

Whip the remaining cream again, if necessary, and, using a wide palette knife, mask the whole of the gateau. It does not need to be very smooth – as long as you achieve a thin layer of cream all over. Set the gateau aside to firm up, in a fridge if possible.

Meanwhile, make the chocolate caraque (curls) to decorate the gateau. (You can cut a corner at this point by surrounding the sides of the gateau with thin rectangles or squares of plain chocolate – some specialist chocolate shops sell these. Large chocolate drops can also be attractive.) Put the chocolate into a small heat-proof bowl. Set over a pan of simmering water and stir until melted. A flat hard surface is needed now – marble is ideal but I use a large laminated chopping board. Wipe the surface lightly with a tissue dipped in vegetable oil. Pour the melted chocolate over the surface and spread it out fairly thinly. Leave to set until no longer sticky to the touch.

To make long curls, hold a sharp knife at an angle and push the blade away from yourself across the surface of the chocolate. Some people use a clean wallpaper stripper for this job and the result is somewhat similar. If the chocolate shatters into crumbs, it is too hard; soften it up again by leaving the board in a warm room. If the chocolate gathers up the knife, it is too soft; leave it to set a little longer.

Drop the chocolate curls straight onto the gateau. (I like to pile them up on top.) Cover the sides of the gateau using the chocolate crumbs. You can, if you like, finish the top with whirls of whipped cream, using a piping bag fitted with a ½ inch (1 cm) star nozzle. Chill before serving.

Eat on the day the gateau is assembled, or freeze for up to a month. Store the unfilled sponge in an airtight tin for up to 2 days, or freeze for up to 1 month.

White Chocolate Ramekins with Dark Chocolate Sauce

1 teasp. brandy
4 dessertsps. strong, hot
  black coffee
3 oz (75g) plain (quality)
  chocolate
9 oz (250 g) white (quality)
  chocolate
1 oz (25 g) unsalted butter
5 fl oz (¼ pint) double
  cream

Grease six small ramekins with butter and dust with plain flour. Knock out any loose flour which does not stick to the butter. Put a pyrex bowl over a pan of simmering water and gently melt the white chocolate. In another bowl whip the cream until floppy. Fold the melted white chocolate into the cream. Divide this mixture between the six ramekins and place them in the freezer.

To make the dark chocolate sauce melt it in the same way in a pyrex bowl. Beat the butter into the chocolate. Add the coffee and the brandy and just a little water to get a pouring consistency.

To serve the tiny rich puddings unmould them by dipping the bottom of each ramekin in hot water. Run a knife round the sides and place each one on a plate. Pour a little dark chocolate sauce round the base of each white chocolate circle.

Mandarin and Grape Flan

SERVES 8

A little solid vegetable oil,
melted
3 large eggs
3 oz (75 g) vanilla sugar
3 oz (75 g) plain white
flour, sifted
2 tblsp. sherry
1 small can mandarin
oranges, drained
4 oz (125 g) seedless green
grapes, or halved and de-
seeded green grapes
2 tblsp. redcurrant jelly
¼ pint (150 ml) double
cream (optional)

Use the melted vegetable oil to grease a 5 inch (20 cm) shallow flan ring with a raised base. Cut two circles of greaseproof paper and fit one to the raised base. Cut the centre out of the other circle so that you are left with a narrow band of paper, and lay this in the bottom of the flan ring. Preheat the oven to moderate, Gas 3, 325°F, 160°C.

Using an electric mixer, or hand held mixer, whip the eggs and sugar together until you have a billowy mass of fluff. (It will take a good 5 minutes with a machine and 10 - 15 minutes by hand.)

Using a sieve, sprinkle about one-third of the flour over the egg mixture and fold this in carefully and quickly with a spatula. Repeat this twice, when you should have a very firm fluffy mixture.

Fill the flan ring about three-quarters full with the mixture and set the flan on a baking tray before putting it into the oven. Bake for about 30 minutes.

Allow the flan to cool a little then run a knife round the outer and inner circles to release it. Peel off the lining paper and cool on a wire tray.

When cold, set the flan on a flat serving plate, put the sherry in a small jug and dribble it over the flan. Arrange the fruit in a pattern, packing it very tightly.

Melt the redcurrant jelly in a small bowl in a pan of simmerig water. Brush the jelly over the fruit, making sure to get into all the corners. Allow to set, then decorate with whipped cream if you wish.

Eat on the day the flan is assembled. I do not like this frozen. The unfilled sponge will keep in an airtight tin for a week, or freeze for up to 1 month.

Meringues

Some chefs still maintain that the best way to achieve a large volume of billowing fluffy egg whites is with a hand-held balloon whisk in a wide copper bowl. You can still get them in some very posh kitchen shops where no-one knows anything about cooking. I use my large Kenwood mixer with a wire whisk and a stainless steel bowl. Glass, china and pottery bowls are all good, but do not use a plastic one since their surface "hold" invisible microscopic dots of fat or oil which work against the egg whites.

Golden rules: 1 – Use large eggs which are at least one week old. New egg whites give much less volume. 2 – Use castor sugar for whitish meringues and light, soft brown sugar for caramel ones. 3 – Whip the egg whites until they are so stiff that they stand up in peaks.

Grease the baking sheets first then line with non-stick paper. This is so that the paper is anchored and it is easy to shape the meringues by hand. Not everyone likes piping bags and nozzles. It is perfectly easy to shape the meringues with a spoon and a spatula.

Small meringues, when cold, can be dipped in melted chocolate and sandwiched together with thick whipped cream. Make meringue baskets by piping or shaping a circle of meringue and adding a shallow wall. Use a half inch (1 cm) pipe. From the full quantity of basic recipe you should get about 11 baskets or 18 small round meringues.

The baskets can be filled with whipped cream and topped with soft fruit. A favourite filling of mine is two large tablespoons of homemade lemon curd folded into a quarter pint of whipped double cream.

Basic Meringue

2 large egg whites
Pinch salt
1 fat pinch cream of tartar
4 oz (125 g) castor sugar

Line baking trays with non-stick paper. Put the egg whites into a large clean grease-free mixing bowl and whisk until frothy. Add the salt and cream of tartar and whip until whites are really stiff. Add the sugar one tablespoon at a time, whisking hard between each addition.

The mixture should be thick and glossy and so stiff that you could easily cut it with a knife. Put the meringue mixture into a large piping bag fitted with a half inch (1 cm) star nozzle and pipe the shapes required onto the baking trays, or shape by hand. Bake the meringues in a very low oven, gas ¼, 225°F, 110°C, for a minimum of 1½ hours. (Ideally meringues should be baked for three hours.) Cool meringues on wire trays. When cold put them immediately into an airtight tin or a tightly-fastened plastic bag.

Floating Islands with Caramel

SERVES 6

1 pint (600 ml) milk
2 large eggs, separated
2 oz (50 g) castor sugar
1 level tblsp. cornflour
Vanilla essence
A little water
2 extra level teasp. castor
* sugar*

Caramel to decorate:
5 oz (150 g) granulated
* sugar*
1 tblsp. water

Pour the milk into a wide saucepan and heat to simmering point. Whisk one egg white until stiff, add 1 oz (25 g) of the sugar and whisk again. Whisk in the other oz of sugar so that the mixture is really firm.

Divide the mixture into six portions and spoon each portion onto the top of the milk (you may have to do this in two batches). Poach until meringue is set, about 4 to 5 minutes in all. Lift onto greaseproof paper with a draining spoon and allow to cool.

Blend the cornflour, two egg yolks, two teaspoons of sugar and a few drops of vanilla essence with enough water to make a thin paste. Slowly stir this into the milk in which the meringue was poached. Return the pan to the heat and stir as it thickens but do not let it boil hard. Cool a little and pour into six glass dishes and place one egg island on top of each.

Caramel:
Put the sugar and water in a heavy-based pan over a high heat. Shake the pan rather than stir until the sugar is dissolved. When the caramel is pale gold watch it carefully until it turns a dark caramel colour, then remove from the heat and allow to stand a little while. Dribble the caramel in a thin stream over each island.

Pavlova

SERVES 12

6 large egg whites
1 pinch salt
12 oz (325 g) castor sugar
1½ teasp. cornflour
1½ teasp. vanilla essence
1½ teasp. vinegar
½ pint (300 ml) double
  cream, whipped
Fresh fruit: strawberries,
  raspberries, grapes, or
  your choice

Line a large baking tray with non-stick paper and draw on it a circle 9 inches (23 cm) across. A dinner plate will help. Pre-heat the oven to gas 1, 275°F, 140°C. Put the egg whites and salt into an electric mixer and whip at high speed until the egg whites are very stiff, or whip with a large loop whisk. With the machine running add the sugar two tablespoons at a time, whipping well between each addition until all sugar is incorporated.

The mixture should be very stiff. Take the bowl away from the machine and quickly fold in the cornflour, vanilla essence and vinegar. Pile the meringue onto the circle on the baking tray. Shape the meringue into a giant nest. Use a skewer to make swirls all round and pull the meringue out in little peaks. Bake for about an hour and a half, when the outside should be crisp and the inside soft.

Allow to cool then lift gently onto a large serving plate or tray. Just before serving pile the whipped cream into the centre of the meringue and cover with fruit. Serve cut in wedges.

Pomegranates

The arrival of the late-fruiting pomegranate is a sure sign of autumn. Artists and children have always loved them for their elaborate interior design and the long, slow pleasure of picking them clean with the help of a pin.

I have always liked the astringent garnet-like shiny fruits, seeds and all, and associate them with Hallowe'en. It's easy to empty the halved fruit. Just turn them inside out over a bowl. Pick out every speck of bitter yellow membrane which encloses the bright seeds, which freeze extremely well in plastic bags.

Pomegranate juice is the basis of the French Grenadine syrup which is used in cocktails. I find it far too sweet for my taste. The ice cream I made with the fresh juice was not too successful. The delicate flavour was almost lost. Far better is the lovely unsweetened water ice below. Serve this like a sorbet on its own between the starter and the main course or with a good vanilla ice cream, one scoop of each and top with the red fruits.

Pomegranate Refresher

This is a very unusual and refreshing long drink which is also good with a dash of vodka or gin.

8 pomegrantes, freshly
  squeezed (20 fl ozs)
2 tblsp. freshly squeezed
  lemon juice
4 to 5 level tblsp. castor
  sugar
Crushed ice to measure up
  the ¾ pint mark in
  jug

Use a large jug to dissolve the sugar in the juices. Just before serving, add the crushed ice and stir well.

Pomegranate Water Ice

4 pomegrantes
Juice of 1 small orange
Water
1 heaped teasp. gelatine
* powder*

Using a lemon squeezer, take the juice from all but one half pomegranate and remove the fruit from this half and set aside. You should have about 10 fluid ounces (half pint) of juice. Squeeze the juice from the orange and make this up to five fluid ounces (quarter pint) with water. Put the orange mixture into a pan, sprinkle the gelatine over the top and allow to soften for five minutes.

Heat gently and stir until the gelatine dissolves. Add the pomegranate juice. Stir well and pour into a large bowl. Put the bowl into the freezer for one hour, or until the ice is at the slushy stage. Use a loop whisk and beat the mixture hard. Return the bowl to the freezer. Repeat the beating every 30 minutes until you get a fine smooth texture (you can use a food processor if you wish).

Pour the ice into a plastic box, cover and leave in the freezer until needed. Remember to remove the ice from the freezer to the fridge 20 minutes before serving to allow the ice to soften a little.

Marinaded and Grilled Lamb Chops

SERVES 4

*8 loin chops, very well
    trimmed of fat*
*6 ozs (175 g) onions, peeled
    and sliced finely*
*1 small clove of garlic,
    peeled and crushed*
*1 dessertsp. black pepper
    corns, crushed*
*5 fl ozs (¼ pint) lamb stock
    from a cube*
2 pomegranates

Put the chops in a single layer in a flat dish. Empty the fruit from one half pomegranate and set aside. Squeeze the juice from the others and pour into a jug. Add the other ingredients, except the lamb stock, and stir well. Pour over the chops. Stand for several hours, or overnight, turning the chops often.

See that the grill is very hot and cook the chops until well browned on each side, but still pink and juicy in the middle. Meanwhile, strain the marinade into a small pan and add the lamb stock. Boil to reduce the liquid. Adjust the seasoning and serve with the chops and the pomegranate fruits scattered over.

Nuts

It is a hard fact for the enthusiastic cook that the long way round is often the best. I'm thinking of bought horseradish sauce which has completely lost its true flavour, and an apple pie whose apples came from a tin.

Nuts come into this category too; coconuts, almonds, hazelnuts and peanuts are all infinitely better, more moist and delicious if shelled and used fresh. To buy a nice coconut pick one which feels heavy and sounds as if it's full of liquid. Pierce two of the dark eyes and pour out the clear juice and set it aside. Crack the nut with a heavy hammer, or crash it down on a strong doorstep, and break into manageable pieces.

Grate these rounded pieces on a round grating tin. Stop before you get to the brown inner skin or use a food processor, but cut away all the brown skin before you start. The delicious grated coconut is miles better than any packet variety.

One way of restoring very dry almonds and cashew nuts is to soak them in water overnight. Remember to use them fairly quickly or they will go rancid. Store pieces of fresh coconut in their own liquid in the fridge.

Fresh Coconut and Pistachio Ice Cream

1½ oz (40 g) pistachio nuts
2 medium-sized eggs,
* separated*
2 oz (50 g) soft brown sugar
5 fl oz double cream
2 oz (50 g) fresh coconut
2 drops pale green food
* colouring (optional)*

Pour boiling water over the nuts and allow to stand until the skins slip off. Dry well and chop small to show green colour. Whisk the egg whites until stiff. Add sugar and whisk again.

In another bowl whisk cream until very thick. In yet another bowl beat egg yolks. Fold the contents of the three bowls together with the green colouring if used. Lastly fold in all but two teaspoons of the nuts and the coconut. Spoon into individual strong glass containers or small souffle dishes. Level the surface and sprinkle on the reserve nuts.

Freeze and remember to remove from the freezer to the fridge for 10 to 15 minutes before serving to allow the texture to soften a little. Serve with a crisp biscuit.

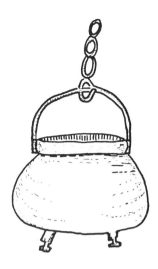

Chicken Kebabs and Peanut Sauce

*2 chicken breasts, boned
and skinned and cut into
one inch cubes*

Marinade:
*2 tblsp. oil
2 tblsp. hot water
1 tblsp. soy sauce
1 tblsp. fresh lemon juice
1/4 teasp. turmeric*

Peanut sauce:
*12 oz (350 g) peanuts in
shell (or 6 oz (175 g)
shelled)
1/4 teasp. chilli powder
2 tblsp. finely chopped
onions
2 tblsp. soy sauce
1 tblsp. brown sugar
1 level teasp. salt
1 tblsp. oil
4 fl oz (125 ml) water*

Garnish:
Lime or lemon wedges

Thread the chopped chicken on to skewers. Do do not pack too tightly. In a shallow dish mix all the ingredients for the marinade and lay the kebabs in the dish for several hours. Spoon the marinade over the chicken every now and then.

Shell the peanuts and roast them in a hot oven until the skins are brown and papery. Rub the nuts together in an old tea towel to remove most of the skins. Put the toasted nuts and all the other ingredients, except the water and oil, in a blender until it becomes a paste.

Put the oil in a small frying pan and scrape the peanut mixture into it. Fry gently, spreading the mixture out and turning it over. When oil starts to run, add the water and bring to a boil. Reduce heat and simmer for four to five minutes. Grill the chicken pieces under a low heat, turning often until thoroughly cooked. Serve with rice or noodles and give each guest a pot of hot peanut sauce.

Cashew Nut Curry

8 oz (225 g) cashew nuts
Cold water to cover
8 oz (225 g) onion, peeled
  and finely chopped
1 tblsp. oil
2 inches cinnamon bark
2 green cardamoms
2 cloves
1¼ teasp. ground coriander
1 teasp. ground cumin
  powder
¼ teasp. turmeric powder
1 level teasp. salt
1½ oz (40 g) creamed
  coconut (bought in bars
  in supermarket – looks
  and feels like hard lard)
4 fl oz (125 ml) very hot
  water

Leave the nuts to swell overnight in the cold water. Next day drain and rinse the nuts. Fry the onions gently in the oil until lightly browned. Use a pestle and mortar to grind down the cinnamon, cardamoms and cloves. Add these spices to the cooking onions and stir well.

In a small bowl dissolve the creamed coconut in the hot water and add this liquid to the pan as well. Do not worry if the creamed coconut is still in pieces, it will soon melt down. Cover the frying pan and simmer the sauce for about 10 minutes until it is thickish. Stir in the Cashew nuts. Serve hot with hot rice.

A BOOK OF GRACES

Compiled by Carolyn Martin

Reproduced by permission of Hodder & Stoughton

GRACE AFTER DINNER

Thank God for dirty dishes
They have a tale to tell
Whilst other folks go hungry
We've eaten very well
For home, wealth and happiness
We shouldn't make a fuss
For by this pile of evidence
God's been very good to us.

Mrs Linda Archer

GRACE SAID AT CRICK WOMEN'S INSTITUTE

Lord Bless this food upon these dishes
As Thou didst bless the loaves and fishes
And like the sugar in the tea
May all of us be stirred by Thee.

Tributed to Miss Marjery L. Collett

"God's Grace is the only Grace,
And all Grace is the Grace of God."

This happy meal will happier be
If we Oh Lord, remember thee.

Mrs Mabel E. Parham

MILLER'S GRACE

Back of the bread is the flour,
Back of the flour is the mill,
And back of the mill is the wind and the rain
And the Father's will.

Tributed to Miss E. J. Allen-Williams

WOMEN'S INSTITUTE CHRISTMAS GRACE

For holly's cheerful crimson berry,
For children's faces shining merry,
For all our loved ones gathered here
For absent loved ones far and near
For food to hearten us in eating
For wine to gladden us in drinking
For love, for health, for happiness
For joy and faith and hope of peace
For countless other gifts beside
We thank thee Lord this Christmas tide.

Mrs Bee Salsbury

PERTHSHIRE CHILDREN'S GRACE

Doon head
Up paws
Thank God
We've jaws.
Amen.

Tributed to Ms A. Methuen

A GRACE FROM A SCILLY ISLAND FISHERMAN

The Lord be praised
My belly's raised
An inch above the table
And I'll be damned
If I'm not crammed
As full as I am able

Mrs K. Middleton

AN OLD SCOTTISH GRACE

Stick in till you stick oot.

M. B. Mavor, Headmaster, Gordonstoun School

AFTER GRACE –
ROBERT BURNS AT THE GLOBE TAVERN, DUMFRIES

O Lord, since we have feasted thus
Which we do so little merit
Let Meg now take away the flesh
And Jock bring in the Spirit.
Amen

A MODERN GRACE

God Bless this bunch
As we munch our lunch.

Contributed by Bishop of Salisbury who got it from his 4 year-old grand-daughter

HODG'S GRACE

Probably dating from the time of the agricultural distress in C19th

Heavenly Father Bless us
And keep us all alive
There's ten of us to dinner
And not enough for five.

THE DRESSED HERRING
The Traditional First-Footing Gift Presented at Hogmanay, and Unique to Dundee

The Red Herrings chosen for Dressing were round and about nine inches long. To preserve them for up to a year they were not gutted but pickled and smoked hard. The fish was first wrapped in newspaper to catch any natural oil, over the newspaper a frill of coloured crepe paper was gathered to make a dress. The dress covered the entire fish. Often, a fancy bonnet was added so that the fish looked like a little old lady.

If you were given a Dressed Herring at Hogmanay, luck would stay with you throughout the coming year.

25th September 1990

Ms Jean Muir, Designer,
Jean Muir Ltd.,
59/61 Farringdon Road
LONDON
EC1M 3HD

Dear Ms. Muir,

Have you ever dressed a herring?

The City of Dundee is celebrating its 800th Birthday in 1991 and we are planning to launch it with the Hogmanay Spectacular on December 31st, 1990. As you know, the last day of the year is called Hogmanay and is a traditional observance in Scotland from earliest times.

Among the customs associated with New Year is "First Footing." This involves visiting your friends in their homes to wish them a good New Year and give them a piece of coal symbolising heat and comfort and also in Dundee, a Dressed Herring.

The tradition of dressing herrings in colourful crepe paper dresses and bonnets for use as First Footing gifts is a tradition unique to Dundee which we hope to have available from barrows in the City Centre.

We realise how very busy you are and hope this is not too much of an imposition on your time. We would of course be delighted if you joined us at Hogmanay and saw your fish suitably enshrined.

Sincerely yours,

HENNY KING (Miss)
Director, Dundee 800

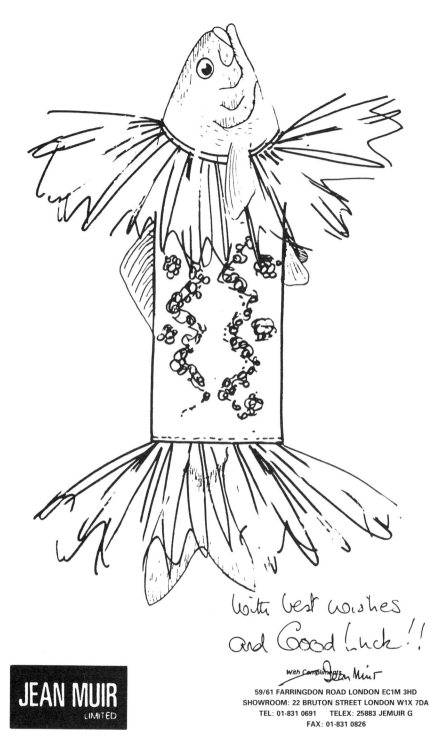

With best wishes
and Good Luck!!

With Compliments   Jean Muir

JEAN MUIR LIMITED

59/61 FARRINGDON ROAD LONDON EC1M 3HD
SHOWROOM: 22 BRUTON STREET LONDON W1X 7DA
TEL: 01-831 0691   TELEX: 25883 JEMUIR G
FAX: 01-831 0826

DUNDEE FOOD FACTS & FIGURES OF THE PAST

Scottish rivers were once so rich in salmon that this fish was available for rich and poor alike.

In Glasgow at one time, apprentices went on strike because they were getting too much salmon.

Fish were among the many exports from Dundee and to preserve them they were salted. For this important export nothing but the best was good enough so salt of a fine quality was imported from the Bay of Biscay region.

During winter, fresh meat was scarce as stocks were killed off because of the shortages of feeding. To augment the salted meat, the Laird had fish from his fish pond and fresh pigeons from his doo-cot or pigeon house. Many of these structures, all of individual design, can still be seen in Angus and Fife. The normal size of a doo-cot could accommodate 400 breeding pairs of birds.

Almost unique or exclusive to Angus and Fife were bee-boles for holding beehives of the "Rusky" type, plaited construction boundary and other stone walls had cupboard-like openings with a stone shelf to support the hive. Honey was important as a source of sweetening, and beeswax was in demand for church candles in the great abbeys of the area.

The rabbit was deliberately introduced north of the Tay in the 19th century. To encourage breeding, man-made warrens were constructed and protective measures taken to prevent unauthorised killing.

Oatmeal was a staple grain and appeared as porridge, brose and cakes. For production of the latter an iron girdle, made in Culross in Fife, became almost essential.

To sup one's porridge, the women folk would find their green horn spoons on the haik or hanging wooden cupboard on the wall. The men carried their horn spoons in their blue bonnets, the latter providing a material to wipe them on after use. Tinkers made horn spoons and guarded the skill.

Household utensils were usually made of wood and included caups (for drinking), luggies (wooden pails or dishes with a handle formed by the projection of one stave above the others). Bickers were also wooden beakers or drinking cups.

The pewter tappit hen, a peculiarly Scottish quart measure of ale or claret, had a hinged lid opened by a thumb-piece. Some had markings vertically arranged down the inside as a measure.

In the Angus Folk Museum in Glamis there is a large caup from Glen Moy designed to accommodate several people supping from it at one time. Each person kept supping to "his ain hole i' the parritch", no trespassing. The caup, or rather its contents, were blessed by the oldest man "crossing it" before the company started eating.

Mill workers in Dundee made stiff porridge and put it in a drawer ready to be cut up in to cold portions to take with them as "a piece."

Our present day grocers arose from the "spicers" of medieval times. Spices were extensively used to disguise food, especially meat which was off when served.

Tea was used more for medicinal purposes to begin with. It was expensive and therefore kept in lockable wooden chests. The key for these tea-caddies was kept by the lady of the household. The origin of the "fly-cup" was the unofficial partaking of the beverage.

A grocer in the old Hawkhill of Dundee in the 1890's sold his produce at the undernoted prices, converted to new pence:

7 lb of sugar	3½p
Tea	5 - 10p / lb
Tea & Digestive Biscuit	3p / lb
Whisky	15p / bottle
"Long-Sleeves" or bottle of	
Tuppenny (table-beers)	9p / dozen

These prices of course must be viewed against the wages of the time. The same young grocer was then earning 6/- a week (old money) for the following hours:

Monday, Tuesday & Wednesday	0800 - 2100
Saturday (no half day)	0800 - 2300
Thursday, Friday	0800 - 2000

Talking of food reminds us that there was once an apt description relative to over-eating: it was "yule-hole", the last hole to which a man could stretch his belt at a yule-tide feast.

The recipes in this book could well lead to a revival of this ancient practice.

James D. Boyd, OBE, FMA, DA, FSA(Scot)

DUNDEE'S EIGHT HUNDRED YEARS

12th Century   **1191** - Granted its first charter as a Royal Burgh by King William the Lion.

1190-91 - Parish Church of St. Mary's founded by David, Earl of Huntingdon.

13th Century   **1296** - Town captured by Edward I, who put the Burgh to fire and sword and destroyed its records and charters.

1298 - Dundonian Alexander Carron, William Wallace's Royal Standard Bearer, was rewarded for his efforts in recapturing The Castle of Dundee with the hereditary office of "Constable of Dundee." In a writ from Wallace, Carron was to be known as "The Skirmisher" from which the family name Scrimgeour derived.

14th Century   **1309** - Robert the Bruce proclaimed the King of Scots in the Greyfriars Monastery in Dundee.

1313 - Dundee Castle recaptured by King Robert as part of his campaign to free Scotland.

1336 - Dundee burnt again when Edward III invaded in an attempt to place Balliol on the Scottish throne.

1385 - The English were back in Dundee looting and burning. It would take a great many years to rebuild the town and church following the ravages of the long Wars of Independence.

15th Century   **1470** - Hector Boece, one of Dundee's outstanding sons, was born. In 1526 he published his "Chronicles of Scotland" which is one of the earliest Scottish Histories.

1482 - St. Mary's Tower - or "Old Steeple" built. It has stood ever since, being extensively repaired and restored in the 19th century.

16th Century   **1564** - Mary Queen of Scots granted the gardens of the former Greyfriars Monastery to the people of Dundee as burial grounds. These were called The Howff – an old Scots word for a meeting place.

1567 - Town fined 2000 merks for supporting the Reformed Church. Earned the nickname "Geneva of the North" due to the leading role it played in the religious struggles of the Reformation.

17th Century   **1645** - Captured by the Marquis of Montrose, then sacked and burned.

1651 - Siege by Cromwell's army under General Monk, when most of the town was destroyed and 1200 inhabitants massacred.

1669 - Grissell Jaffray burned for witchcraft in the Seagate.

18th Century **1746** - Freedom of the Burgh granted to the Duke of Cumberland after his victory at Culloden.

1763 - Founding of Dundee's first bank by George Dempster of Dunnichen.

1793 - First attempts made to spin flax by machine. Coarse and heavy linen became the mainstay of Dundee's wealth.

1797 - Keiller factory established, producing the famous Dundee marmalade.

19th Century **1825-1832** - First experiments made with jute from India. By the second half of the century the jute industry had become central to the town's economy, earning it the name "Juteopolis."

1832 - One of Scotland's earliest railways opened, linking the town with Newtyle.

1838 - Adhesive postage stamp invented by James Chalmers.

1879 - Tay Bridge disaster. 75 dead.

1889 - Granted a Royal Charter by Queen Victoria conferring on the old Burgh the status and dignity of a city.

20th Century **1901** - Captain Scott's Antarctic research ship "Discovery" launched. 1620 tons and the strongest wooden vessel ever built.

1937 - The Famous "Beano" comic launched by D. C. Thomson.

1966 - Tay Road Bridge opened.

1967 - University of Dundee acquired its Royal Charter.